VOICES OF CHANGE:
Southern Pulitzer Winners

Maurine Hoffman Beasley
Richard R. Harlow
University of Maryland

University Press
of America™

Library of Congress Catalog Card Number: 79-52511

To our respective spouses, Hank and Mary, for their patience and encouragement.

The body copy of this book was typeset on the INCO, INC. RP-8080 microprocessor. (INCO, INC., 7916 Westpark Drive, McLean, Virginia 22102.)

TABLE OF CONTENTS

CHAPTER 1	VOICES OF CHANGE		1
CHAPTER 2	W. HORACE CARTER *Tabor City (N.C.) Tribune*		7
CHAPTER 3	CARO BROWN *Alice (Tex.) Echo*		31
CHAPTER 4	BUFORD BOONE *Tuscaloosa (Ala.) News*		49
CHAPTER 5	IRA B. HARKEY, JR. *Pascagoula (Miss.) Chronicle*		65
CHAPTER 6	HAZEL BRANNON SMITH *Lexington (Miss.) Advertiser*		83
CHAPTER 7	JOHN R. HARRISON *Gainesville (Fla.) Sun*		97
CHAPTER 8	HORANCE G. DAVIS *Gainesville (Fla.) Sun*		115
APPENDIX A	SOUTHERN PULITZER WINNERS		132
APPENDIX B	SELECTED ANNOTATED BIBLIOGRAPHY		137
	NOTES		141
	INDEX		143

ACKNOWLEDGEMENT

Every book seems to need a host of people to assist at its birth. This one is no exception. First we must acknowledge the encouragement of Dean Ray E. Heibert and Dr. L. John Martin of the University of Maryland College of Journalism. Their support and advice were invaluable during some of our most discouraging moments. Our appreciation goes also to the Dean of Undergraduate Studies, Dr. Robert E. Shoenberg, under whose auspices our research was conducted. Without the instructional grants from his office, this effort could not have been completed. In addition, our thanks to the National Newspaper Association for its grant which helped us complete the project.

Also there are individual contributions to be recognized: Betty Garner for the many hours she spent transcribing some woefully inaudible tapes as well as attending to the administrative details associated with our grants; Aura Marazzi for keying the final manuscript into the word processor; and Curt Adkins for his conscientious editing. And our special thanks to Dr. Caroline Barnard Hall, of New Orleans, for her interview with Ira Harkey.

We also extend posthumous recognition to Dr. Otho Beall of the University of Maryland American Studies Program for bringing the authors together in what has been a mutually rewarding and educational experience. Our thanks also to Rita Popp of Northern Illinois University for helping with the bibliography.

We must not overlook INCO, INC. of McLean, Virginia, Harlow's employer, for allowing one-half of the writing team occasional absences from his office to pursue research on this book.

Finally our deep appreciation to all the Pulitzer Prize winners we interviewed who generously shared with us their time and experiences. We started our research with a question, "What did you _do_...? We finished knowing what they _are_: Proud and courageous members of the Fourth Estate.

M.B.
R.R.H.

Maurine Hoffman Beasley is an assistant professor of journalism at the University of Maryland College of Journalism. She holds Bachelors' degrees in history and journalism from the University of Missouri, a Master's degree in journalism from Columbia University and a Ph.D. in American Civilization from George Washington University. Prior to teaching, she was a staff writer for the _Kansas City_ (Mo.) _Star_ and the _Washington Post_. She is co-author of _Women in the Media: A Documentary Sourcebook_.

Richard R. Harlow is manager of the Technical Publications Department at INCO, INC., McLean, Virginia. He holds a Bachelor's degree in English from Bridgewater (Mass.) State College and a Master's in journalism from Boston University. He has taught science communication and journalism at Boston University and Northeastern University and in several industrial and government communication programs. He is also a free-lance writer and frequent contributor to newspapers, trade, and technical journals. He is currently a doctoral candidate in the American Studies Program, University of Maryland.

VOICES OF CHANGE

> By composing a severely just account of the War on
> the basis of contemporary evidence - ascertaining
> and testing its facts, combining them in compact
> narrative, and illustrating them by careful analysis
> of the spirit of the press...the author aspires to
> place the history of the War above political misrep-
> resentations, to draw it from disguises and conceal-
> ments, and to make it complete in three departments:
> the record of facts; the accounts of public opinions
> existing with them; and the lessons their context
> should convey or inspire. These three are the just
> elements of history. If the author succeeds in what
> he proposes, he will have no reason to boast that he
> has produced any great literary wonder; but he will
> claim that he has made an important contribution to
> Truth, and done something to satisfy curiosity with-
> out "sensation," and to form public opinion without
> violence.(1)

So wrote Edward A. Pollard, editor of the <u>Richmond (Va.) Examiner</u>,
at the close of the Civil War. Outraged at what he considered the
untruths being published by both sides during and following the conflict,
Pollard, one of the South's first historians, set forth his goal of
cutting through "disguises and concealments." Although the prolific
Pollard himself was a prejudiced and often unjust observer, his stated
intentions summed up the honorable aims of both American journalism and
history.

While socially responsible journalism in the United States is
dedicated to providing information of immediate utility, history provides
what Carl L. Becker called the study of "the selfconsciousness of
humanity."(2) Both fields deal with reality - as perceived by the
journalist in immediate reaction to events and by the historian from a
vantage point of time and studied reflection. Each generation rewrites
its own history based on current cultural values, yet the task of the
historian remains, as Becker said, to keep history "in reasonable harmony
with what actually happened."(3) Journalism thus becomes the initial
step in the writing of history, and both journalists and historians
endeavor to find the truth that humanity needs to know to make sense of
its world. The history of journalism itself merges the two disciplines
and becomes the study of humanity's consciousness as expressed in the
journalistic report, according to James Carey, president of the
Association for Education in Journalism.(4)

With journalists on the firing line of history, they frequently come
under attack in their efforts to combat what Pollard called
"misrepresentation." The risky business of truth-seeking disturbs the
status quo, and those who engage in it may find themselves excoriated for

1

their pains - bearers of messages that the public refuses to hear. Consequently, history holds many examples of journalists who "played it safe" and failed to contradict prevailing sentiments, even if obvious truths were suppressed in the process.

The history of Southern journalism illustrates this point. Professing to love their land and their culture, the vast majority of Southern journalists declined to speak up for racial justice and compliance with Federal law during the 1950s, '60s and '70s when civil rights struggles dominated the scene. Since the days of Pollard, the Southern press, with few exceptions, had endorsed the concept of white supremacy. Although the post-Civil War South produced distinguished editors - such as Henry W. Grady of the <u>Atlanta Constitution</u> - these individuals fastened their eyes on economic recovery and overlooked the injustices of a rigid racial structure.

Particularly falling prey to prejudice were most segments of the rural and small-town press. Although they preached enlightment in the fields of education and agriculture, they sought to "keep the Negro in his place."(5) Thomas D. Clark, historian of the Southern country press stated, "Almost unanimously the country press declared the South a white man's country. The Negro was said not to be ready to participate in political affairs. He needed education, poise and experience before he could be prepared."(6) Few recommendations, however, were given for this "preparation."

Even those journalists who recognized the inherent fallacy of white supremacy in a democratic society were afraid to voice their views. "In the discussion of the race question, as in that of almost every other public issue, editors realized the limiting factor of their patrons' preconceived opinion," Clark said. "No doubt many papers would have expressed a far more progressive attitude had their publishers felt the public mind was conditioned for it."(7)

This reluctance to oppose prevailing views is reflected in the relatively small number of Southern journalists to win Pulitzer prizes, the nation's most coveted journalistic awards, for their stands on racial questions. A total of 45 Southern newspapers and individual journalists have won Pulitzer prizes in public service, reporting, and editorial writing from 1918, when the annual awards were begun, to 1978. Given by Columbia University, the prizes represent the best-known symbols of journalistic excellence in the United States.(8)

Of the 45 prizes, 18 were given for journalistic accomplishments involving racial issues. When the Ku Klux Klan spread its doctrines of racial bigotry in the 1920's, the <u>Memphis Commercial Appeal</u> and the <u>Columbus</u> (Ga.) <u>Enquirer-Sun</u> (along with the <u>New York World</u>) won Pulitzer prizes for efforts to combat it. Even though the Klan controlled the Georgia state government, Julian LaRose Harris of the <u>Enquirer-Sun</u> found the courage in 1925 to berate the KKK slogan, "It's Great to Be a Georgian," on his editorial page: "Is it great to be a citizen of a state which is the proud parent of a cowardly hooded order founded and fostered by men who have been proved liars, drunkards, blackmailers, and murderers?.... Let each one answer as he will, but the reply of the <u>Enquirer-Sun</u> is no."(9) Harris's editorial policy helped to defeat the

Klan, but it "did little to make the Enquirer-Sun a financial success," according to historians.(10) As the 1920s drew to a close, Grover Cleveland Hall, editor of the Montgomery (Ala.) Advertiser, and Louis Isaac Jaffe, editor of the Norfolk (Va.) Virginian-Pilot, won prizes for crusades against lynching.(11)

Nearly two full decades elapsed before more Southern journalists earned Pulitzer prizes for challenging the status quo of white supremacy. In 1946 Hodding Carter, editor of the 6,500-circulation Delta Democrat-Times of Greenville, Miss., was honored for a series of editorials that attacked racial, religious, and economic bigotry. Two years later, Virginius Dabney of the Richmond (Va.) Times-Dispatch received the prize for editorials that questioned Southern attitudes and opposed the single-party system and poll tax used to deprive blacks of voting rights.

In the 1950s with changing racial patterns impelled by the U.S. Supreme Court, a total of six Pulitzer prizes - the same number that had been awarded in the previous 30 years - were given to Southern editors who attempted to calm racial passions. Two North Carolina weeklies, the Whiteville News Reporter and the Tabor City Tribune, fought a revival of the Ku Klux Klan and won public service awards. Since the papers, which had a combined circulation of less than 10,000, faced loss of advertising and threats against their editors, their campaigns showed exceptional devotion to journalistic responsibility. Each was honored in 1953.

The next year the Supreme Court outlawed segregation in public schools, unleashing a wave of fury across the South as racial supremacists vowed not to obey court orders. When a mob threatened to harm Autherine Lucy, the first black student to be admitted to the University of Alabama, Buford Boone, editor of the Tuscaloosa (Ala.) News, endeavored to bring peace to his community. Boone received the editorial writing prize in 1957. As the desegregation battle reached Little Rock, a mob backed by Governor Orval Faubus forced eight black students to leave a white high school and caused President Eisenhower to order Army paratroopers into the city to uphold the law. In the midst of the turmoil, the Arkansas Gazette provided factual coverage of the crisis. In editorials its editor, Harry S. Ashmore, argued, "...sooner or later we have got to make some adjustment of our legal institutions to comply with the public policy of the United States...."(12) Both Ashmore and the Gazette won Pulitzer prizes in 1958. Ralph McGill, editor of the Atlanta Constitution, was honored in 1959 for editorial writing that attacked politicians who advocated lawlessness in fighting integration.

In the following 11 years five more Southern journalists won for urging racial justice in tense community situations, while a sixth was recognized for a successful campaign to improve housing, primarily for blacks. The editorial writing award in 1960 went to Lenoir Chambers, editor of the Norfolk Virginia-Pilot, for his stand against closing Virginia schools to avoid desegregating them. In Mississippi two editors, Ira B. Harkey Jr. of the Pascagoula Chronicle and Hazel Brannon Smith of the Lexington Advertiser, defied local segregationists and spoke up for civil rights. Harkey, who urged admission of James Meredith, a black, to the University of Mississippi, met violent opposition and sold his newspaper after winning a Pulitzer prize for editorial writing in

1963. The same award went to Smith in 1964 for exposing the bigotry of White Citizens' Councils and upholding the rights of blacks to equal treatment before the law. In 1967 Eugene C. Patterson, editor of the Atlanta Constitution, won for editorial writing attacking racism and political demagoguery, including the failure of the Georgia legislature to seat Julian Bond, a black. The Gainesville (Fla.) Sun produced two other Pulitzer prize winners for editorial writing: John R. Harrison, the publisher, who won in 1965 for a housing code campaign, and Horance G. Davis, an editorial writer, honored in 1971 for calling on the community to accept peaceful school desegregation.

Of the 18 awards given for promoting racial change in the South, fully half went to representatives of the community press (newspapers with less than 35,000 circulation).(13) These included the awards to the anti-Klan Columbus (Ga.) Enquirer-Sun and two North Carolina weeklies, the Whiteville News Reporter and the Tabor City Tribune; Buford Boone, Ira B. Harkey Jr. and Hazel Brannon Smith, all of whom opposed violent segregationists; and the two winners from the Gainesville Sun, John R. Harrison and Horance G. Davis.

These awards denoted unusual journalistic courage since most small newspapers stand to lose more than their metropolitan counterparts by taking controversial stands. Social scientists have pointed out that the power structure of small communities, operating through informal contacts between leaders, tends to discourage open discussions of policy in local newspapers.(14) Morris Janowitz, in his study of community newspapers within Chicago, found that personal contacts between publishers and community leaders and the publishers' need to gain advertising support from businesses influences the community press to maintain the status quo.(15)

Mass communications researchers concluded that newspapers in small communities are likely to serve a "maintenance" function in contrast to newspapers in large communities which more actively encourage public dialogue.(16) This may stem from the unwillingness of many residents of small communities to tolerate the disruption of social change, according to other researchers.(17) Indeed, journalism history is filled with examples of editors who defied the community power structure and soon found themselves without newspapers.(18) As a result, community newspapers frequently have declined to print controversial editorials and have been attacked for being "lily-livered."(19) Some small-town editors have gone so far as to urge their counterparts to "censor" news that "tears down" the communities.(20)

In view of these attitudes, the achievements of the Pulitzer prize winners from small papers who refused to bow to reactionary pressure stand out as examples of journalistic valor. Although they found it both economically and physically perilous to take unpopular positions on civil rights, they stood up for what they knew was inevitable - and what they believed was right. As might be expected, the smaller and weaker their publications, the more crippling the reprisals, which ranged from cancellation of subscriptions and establishment of competing newspapers to threats against their lives. Because these men and women refused to give in to mob violence and to upholding a waning caste system, they became the voices of change in the South - voices that have led that region into its current period of economic and social growth.

This book introduces seven Pulitzer-prize winners from the community press who recognized the inevitability of social change and found the courage to tell their readers the truth at a crucial period in Southern history. Six won for their stands on issues involving black-white relations during the last quarter-century of civil rights struggle. A seventh, Caro Brown, of the Alice (Tex.) Echo, is included because she reported on another aspect of Southern change - attempts to free Mexican-American voters from political bosses. Brown won a Pulitzer prize in 1955 for reporting a complicated series of court inquiries into the affairs of George B. Parr, who controlled a bloc of Mexican-American voters.

Using an oral history approach based on personal interviews with these prize winners, this book marks the first effort to record the recollections of a group of distinguished Southern journalists from the community press. It is intended to inspire as well as enlighten - to prompt others to follow them as well as to tell "how" and "why" these individuals made their mark on journalism history and, in turn, on their respective localities. The interview with each winner is followed by examples of his or her prize-winning work.

Those that really say something...are putting
their future on the line every week.

W. HORACE CARTER
Tabor City (N.C.) Tribune
Pulitzer Prize—Public Service
1953

2

Preaching its doctrine of hatred and violence, the Ku Klux Klan rode again in rural counties along the North-South Carolina border in the early 1950s. Fueled by the approach of desegregation and the feverish anti-Communist witch-hunting of the McCarthy era, it appealed to thousands who sought both excitement and a vehicle to attack those perceived as "enemies."

As bands of night riders gathered for cross-burnings, an era of floggings, threats and brutality began. With many local officials themselves Klan members, few residents of Horry County, South Carolina, or adjoining Columbus Country, North Carolina, found the fortitude to denounce Klan activity. Afraid of physical injury or economic loss, most kept silent and the terrorism continued.

One of the few in Columbus County to take a firm stand against the Klan was W. Horace Carter, editor of the struggling <u>Tabor City Tribune</u>, a weekly newspaper with less than 2,000 circulation in a small tobacco town near the South Carolina border. "In this democratic country, there's no place for an organization of the caliber of the Ku Klux Klan which made a scheduled parade through our streets last Saturday night," Carter wrote in a front-page editorial on July 26, 1950.

A North Carolina native, Carter conceded that he agreed with some of the objectives of the Klan, including its stands against communism and immorality. But he vehemently opposed mob rule in place of law. Although he lost badly needed advertising revenue, he kept up his campaign against the Klan for three years in the face of violence against Columbus residents.

7

Also fighting against the Klan was the semi-weekly <u>News Reporter</u> of Whiteville, the county seat of Columbus County. Even though its circulation declined from 6,000 to 4,500, the paper, edited by Willard Cole, maintained its anti-Klan stand.

The Klan's "invisible empire" crumbled rapidly in 1952 after FBI agents and state investigators conducted investigations that led to prison sentences for 18 Klan members including the "Grand Dragon," Thomas L. Hamilton. As part of his campaign Carter wrote an "open-letter" editorial to Hamilton answering Hamilton's letter to him.

In 1953, the <u>News Reporter</u> and the <u>Tabor City Tribune</u> jointly were awarded the Pulitzer prize for public service. Cole, now dead, left the <u>News Reporter</u> after the prize was bestowed and went into public relations work. Carter acquired other weeklies and then moved into the paper products business.

Born in 1921 in Albemarle, N.C., Carter worked his way through journalism school at the University of North Carolina and served as a lieutenant in the U.S. Navy during World War II. In 1946 he went to Tabor City and started the <u>Tabor City Tribune</u>.

His stand against the Ku Klux Klan brought him 27 honors from the Sidney Hillman Foundation, the North Carolina Press Association, the National Editorial Association and other organizations. In 1953 he was named the North Carolina Young Man of the Year by Jaycees and the next year he was selected as one of the Jaycees' ten outstanding Young Men of America.

"I've spent half my time since I came to Tabor City on civic affairs," Carter said. He has been mayor of Tabor City, president of the Rotary Club, president of the Columbus County Economic Development Committee and a trustee of the county library. For 17 years he headed Tabor Industrial Enterprises, a municipal group seeking industry for Tabor City.

Now semi-retired, Carter remains secretary-treasurer of his business, the Atlantic Publishing Co. As editor-emeritus of the <u>Tabor City Tribune</u>, he continues to write a weekly column. The parents of three children, he and his wife, Lucille, divide their time between Tabor City and Hawthorne, Florida, where Carter fishes and writes articles for outdoor magazines.

CARTER INTERVIEW

Question: What was Tabor city like in the late 1940s when you first went there?

Carter: Tabor City was a little tobacco town of less than 2,000 people when I went there in 1946, and it was a produce-growing center--strawberries, snapbeans, sweet corn, white potatoes--but tobacco was our primary money crop. We had no industry there.

Question: Why did you decide to go there and start a newspaper?

Carter: Well, my wife and I had been married something over a year. I had just got out of four years in the Navy. I was a navigator during the war and we had a six weeks' old baby and I had finished the University of North Carolina at Chapel Hill, and I went to Tabor City because of two things. First I had an uncle who was a Baptist preacher there who had acquainted me with the town some years before that because he had a son the same age that I was. My family used to spend some time down there with him in the summer and I can remember that even in the barber shops (and I must have been 12 or 14) I heard persons talk about how they needed a newspaper in Tabor City...and the week that I finished, I picked up a <u>Raleigh News Observer</u> and looked at the classified ads and saw where Tabor City, N.C. was advertising for somebody to come and be the executive secretary of its Chamber of Commerce or Merchant's Association. In the same paper was another

9

classified ad asking somebody to come to Tabor City and start a newspaper, so I went down to Tabor City,...130 or 140 miles from Chapel Hill and I applied for both jobs. I wanted the Merchant's Association executive secretary job because I had to have some way of feeding my family, and I wanted to start a newspaper down there as soon as I could. I had no money of consequence, $3,000 or $4,000 that I had saved in the Navy.

Question: Had the town ever had a newspaper?

Carter: They had had a summertime, tobacco-season paper...somebody would just come in and run one, two or three months in the summer when the farmers were bringing tobacco to town and the warehouses were needing an advertising media.... I answered the ad. I kept the Merchant's Association executive secretary job for two weeks and I found a printer who was willing to print the paper for me on halves. He'd get half of the advertising revenue for printing it, I'd get the other half for producing the advertising and the news matter.

Question: And that's how you started what has become Atlantic Publishing Company?

Carter: Yes, that's right. And it grew from there. We now do more business by the day than we did the first year we were in business. Of course, we are now in the commercial printing business, the dye-cutting business, wholesale paper business as well as the weekly newspaper business, but we started with just the <u>Tabor City Tribune</u>.

Question: And you and your wife did all the work?

Carter: We did the janitorial work, the advertising, circulation, and the news. That's right. We finally hired a lady who helped us with a little social news and kept the office when I had to be out selling ads. She worked for us for a long time for $20 or $30 a week. We eventually got a little bit of printing equipment and anybody that's acquainted with how difficult it was to get equipment after World War II can fully respect the chore this was. Even if you had the money, you couldn't buy any kind of printing equipment, it just wasn't available after World War II.

Question: Did your Pulitzer prize culminate three years of editorials campaigning against the Klan?

Carter: Editorial and news coverage, yes. All of our editorials on the Klan crusade were front-page editorials. I suppose the news coverage we gave of the developments had as much to do with the prize as the editorials did. I'd say that over those three years we probably had 24 or 30 editorials on the front page but we also had events that the Klan was involved with: Everything from their recruiting campaign to their parades through town to their public meetings, their cross burnings and eventually to the floggings, and that's what we called all the beating that went on in that period, the floggings of the citizens, where they took people from their homes and beat them up and usually left them unclothed or nearly unclothed some miles from their home....

Question: When did the Klan start?

Carter: The Klan movement began in '47 or '48 during Truman's Administration.

Question: Why was there this resurgence?

Carter: In the first place, Truman was terribly disliked in this part of the South. Truman was a President who was entirely unacceptable to the people in this little rural community. You have to remember that it was in this period that the movement was underway to bring about desegregation of the schools and eventually in '54 came the big decision. There was a lot of movement all over the country to do away with segregation and I think this had something to do with it. I think, though, that the behind-the-scenes reason for the rising of the Klan was the fact that World War II was over. You had a lot of young people--a lot of veterans--back from all over the world who had been shooting and killing and they came back home with not too many things to do and a lot of them got involved with Ku Klux Klan as an adventure. Some of the best friends I have today were veterans sent to the penitentiary for their Klan activity.

Question: Did veterans find at this point that the blacks were demanding more rights than previously?

Carter: I'm sure that had something to do with it but you've got to keep in mind in the same breath that the Ku Klux Klan was more than just an anti-black organization, it was much more. They usually had three, four or five speakers at any public meeting and I went to all their public meetings, and I surmise as many as 27 different things were criticized at a meeting and the Negro was not criticized any more than any of the other 26. He was one of a long list of grievances that the Klan had against the establishment. We've had, as you know, in recent years, particularly in the 1960s, a lot of young people who were anti-establishment. You had anti-establishment in the Ku Klux Klan. Now people still think in terms of it being just a group out to harass the colored, but most of the people flogged and beaten up by the Ku Klux Klan were not blacks, not in our community.

Question: How many people are in the whole county?

Carter: 50,000. Of course it's a big county, the third largest in the state. There's no big town, but a big geographical area and we are on the state line so Horry County, South Carolina, is just as much Tabor City as Columbus County is as far as our little paper is concerned. We had in Columbus county about 1500 members of the Ku Klux Klan. They had 3500 members in Horry County. It had a population at that time of about 60,000. You see this is a pretty good-sized group of people. Getting back to the things, though, that they criticized, the United Nations was always high on the list. They were always very much anti-United Nations and one of the men they criticized at that time was an idol of mine, Dr. Frank P. Graham. He was president of the University of North Carolina. He was criticized all the time by the Klan because they considered him a communist and communism was high on

their list of things they disliked. I believe they emphasized that
more than any other one thing.

Question: Weren't they anti-Jew, and anti-Catholic?

Carter: Yes, yes. Anti-United Nations, anti-Harry S. Truman and
a lot of other things.

Question: Did you start your campaign against the Klan as soon as
it began to resume its activity?

Carter: Before it resumed its activity. Before they had the
first public meeting I had an indication from a good friend that there
was some movement to reorganize the Ku Klux Klan. At that time I wrote
a front-page column every week and I said in this front-page column
that we had no place for vigilantes or any other group that was going
to try to impose its kind of justice on the people outside the law in
Columbus County, Horry County, and Tabor City. We had no need for this
kind of organization. Following that column, the "Grand Dragon" of the
Ku Klux Klan came to see me--that was Thomas L. Hamilton--from
Leesville, South Carolina.

Question: What year was this?

Carter: It was either early in '50 or late in '49. He came to
see me and he was upset over the fact that a little newspaper like us
would set ourselves up as any guidance for the people. He felt that
they did need spokesmen, that they did need an organization to
counteract the communism that was sweeping the country, that the
politicians weren't doing anything about the way the country was being
taken over by the Russian communists. He came to see me two other
times. We obviously were diametrically opposite in our beliefs. He
was always criticizing Dr. Graham when he came to see me and I was
always talking up Dr. Graham. He ran for the U.S. Senate at this same
period and he was beaten by a few votes by a much lesser liberal than
he was. Dr. Graham was thereafter with the United Nations and he was
the United States intermediary to Indonesia. The Klan was always
against him. Hamilton was a 32nd Degree Shriner. He said he was a
church-going man, and a family man, and had all kinds of character
references, but he led that group that formed the Ku Klux Klan. I
always thought he was in it for the money because the Klan got $10 a
membership for everybody they signed up. All the members got for it
was a bed sheet and a white cap, so I figured they were making a lot of
money out of the memberships. These boys that were in the Klan also
had to pay dues, monthly, quarterly, some periodic time. Hamilton
claimed that he wasn't getting a cent out of it. He was in it because
of the idealism of protecting Americans from the communist efforts to
put the races together. He got four years in the penitentiary
eventually and before he served the four years, he said he had been
wrong, that he had made a mistake in ever starting the Ku Klux Klan and
that he was sorry he ever got involved in it. He made those statements
and he was released. The last I heard about him he was a used-car
salesman in Augusta, Georgia.

Question: Did Hamilton threaten you when he came to see you?

Carter: We were threatened not only by Hamilton but...by others. Not just me either, but my wife and children, in this period. We were threatened in just about any way and every way that you can be threatened. I mean from notes put under the windshield wiper on the car, to those that were stuck to my office door and under the door, telephone messages, written messages. Every kind of feasible threat that I can think of, we had during this period. We also had a much more direct threat from economics. A little paper in a little town like we were with no great financial resources operates on a narrow line between a living and bankruptcy...and Hamilton's big threat was always that "we will put you out of business. We'll pressure enough of your advertisers that you won't get any business. We'll pressure enough of your subscribers that nobody will read your paper and you'll be out of business." This was the kind of threat that Hamilton always made. He'd tell me this to my face, but the threats that we were going to be harmed physically, or my family was going to harmed physically, these were a little more subtle. These were the ones that were under my windshield and sticking to my door, and telephone messages about...physical violence,..we had many of these.

Question: What did the notes say?

Carter: "We'll get you one night just like we got the last man that we flogged or the last man and woman that we flogged, you're going to get the same things that they got." And, you see, we were running stories on these incidents every week. "A man and a woman were taken to such-and-such a place and beaten up and they were admitted to the Columbus County Hospital with severe bruises and lacerations." These folks were reluctant to talk but we had the news of these floggings in the paper almost every week.

Question: Why were they flogged?

Carter: Now here comes something that I don't know whether the average person who has studied or knows the Ku Klux Klan knows or not. Generally speaking, the Ku Klux Klan was flogging people on the basis that they were leading immoral lives, not that they were black, or Catholic, or Jewish, although they criticized these groups in their meetings. But the floggings, the beatings that they gave people generally occurred in cases of (unmarried) people living together or of some man who wasn't taking care of his wife or children and was off drunk and running around. These are the kind of people that they beat up and even in the newspaper of that time I repeatedly said that you cannot make any good case for the type of people that were harrassed and flogged--that they deserved some kind of punishment but not this kind--that their punishment, if and when they got any punishment, ought to come through the courts, through the social services, through some kind of organized governmental procedure and not by a bunch of vigilantes. But the people that got beat up in almost every instance were breaking some of the moral laws of the country.

Question: These were not necessarily black people?

Carter: There were more whites than blacks. But there were a few blacks. For instance, in Myrtle Beach, that's a part of Horry County on the coast, the Klan attacked a Negro clerk there on a Saturday night on the grounds that this guy was illegally dispensing alcoholic beverages. They were all masked and hooded and they shot this place up and in the course of this shooting, shooting came the other way too. The blacks inside the night club began firing back and it was a regular war for several hours. During the course of this, one of the Klansmen was shot and killed.... Another Klansmen picked him up and carried him to the hospital with his hood and his robe on. When he got there and they undressed him; he was wearing a policeman's uniform, and he was a policeman in the county seat at Conway, South Carolina. Many of the Klansmen were sheriff's deputies and sheriffs and politicians....

Question: You knew who they were in Tabor City?

Carter: Not entirely. I knew a few of them, just because I knew some people who knew that they had some of their family in the Klan. But generally, I didn't know who they were. One of our own city council members was a Klansman and I didn't know that he was and he was convicted and would have gone to the penitentiary except he died of a heart attack just a week before he started to serve his sentence.

Question: Were you one of the few prominent individuals who had the courage to to speak out against the Klan?

Carter: I don't want any bouquets, but there was almost nobody else in Tabor City who spoke out against the Klan. We had a Methodist minister who at least one time during this three years preached some part of a sermon against the Ku Klux Klan. Our own Baptist minister never mentioned it...and as far as I know, no sermons were being preached against it in the Presbyterian Church.

Question: Why do you think you had the courage to do it?

Carter: I don't see how anybody from the University of North Carolina could feel that there's any group of vigilantes with the right to beat up people. I think that's part of the tradition of Chapel Hill--that we're supposed to protect the rights of people--and I give the University credit for any leaning that I might have in that direction. And, you might keep this in mind, if we had been well off financially, if we had had a nice home and a nice print shop and a fine automobile, maybe I wouldn't have done it. Maybe I wouldn't have campaigned against the Klan because I could have had a lot to lose. I mean I could have lost my newspaper, my home, my car, this kind of thing. But, we didn't have anything. We just had a rented building and a $15 typewriter and a few obsolete pieces of equipment and we fought them on the grounds...that we can't lose anything because we don't have anything and we're going to fight them because we think this is the difference between right and wrong.... We could have had some physical harm, but we didn't. We were always expecting this, though. We lived on edge for a long period of time in a kind of nervous condition and nobody can say that he's just plain brave enough not to let this get to him. I mean there is no such thing as these threats not getting to you after a while. But, you asked the question who supported us in the community--we lacked support. We never had support. I never had the first advertiser ever come to me and say "I'm going to keep on doing business with you even if you keep on writing against the Klan." We lost some advertisement during this campaign and you know, we've got a town with 80 retail businesses to start with all put together, so you can't lose many and stay in business.

Question: How much advertising do you think you actually lost?

Carter: We lost about a fourth of it for a period of like two or three years. The roughest two or three years of our lives. We were living in rented houses, very poor houses, and trying to raise two or three children. We survived it, but if the Klan leaders had not been convicted, if the FBI had not come in and made the original arrest and the state hadn't followed up with a lot of other arrests, and if we hadn't convicted them and put them in the penitentiary, I expect they would have broken us.

Question: When did the FBI come in?

Carter: The FBI got into the case in 1950. They made the original arrest in '51 and it was in 1951 and '52 that they started sending them (the Klansmen) to the penitentiary, 62 of them.

Question: On conspiracy charges?

Carter: Assault and conspiracy to assault, those were the charges. These were the first instances that Ku Klux Klansmen had ever been convicted in the United States for activities relating to the Klan. There had been a few individual Klansmen in the north, some twenty-five years before that, that had been convicted of just plain criminal activities, but they didn't do these crimes under the pretense of Klan activity.

Question: It most have taken an awfully lot of guts for a young man just starting out in business to have written an editorial opposing the Klan before it even got started. You said someone came to you and said the Klan was going to begin. Do you remember how you felt when you first heard that?

Carter: I felt just exactly like I feel right now. I felt that this is just what we <u>don't</u> need. You see our community had been known as razor city; border town. We had a very bad reputation for shootings, cuttings, all kinds of violence, and to me this was the kind of thing that I was there to help overcome. I felt that a good newspaper, even a small one, could help overcome these obstacles. I felt we had the desire, we had the motive, and the reason for trying to make Tabor City a better place to live. I didn't think we could do it with Ku Klux Klansmen running around and shooting up homes and dragging people out and beating them.

16

Question: Do you know who first told you?

Carter: Yes sir. I know just as though he were standing here in front of us. Frank Young was the barber who cut my hair for twenty-some years. He was not necessarily anti-Klan, but he thought I ought to know about it. I told Frank that I'd like the chance to talk to Hamilton, the Grand Dragon. The next day Hamilton was in the office....

Carter: Now the FBI worked very closely with us, too. The FBI insofar as the Klan was concerned was the straw that broke them. They eventually planted informers within the Klan. They knew when the floggings were going to come off. They knew where they were going to come off, and when they made the first arrest, it was a very well-synchronized thing in which they...just swooped down on a lot of people in different areas and at the same time arrested them all instantly, carried them to Fayetteville N.C. Federal Court, and had them indicted and in jail almost before local authorities knew anything about what was going on. And that was the way to do it because the local authorities you couldn't trust.... The FBI ought to have all the credit there is for breaking up the Klan in North and South Carolina.... But, you know, the FBI never arrested people just simply because they belonged to the Klan. They made the arrests because they broke the law with assault or conspiracy to assault. Nobody was arrested simply because he was a member.

Question: How much impact do you think your campaign had?

Carter: I have always believed that we got a great deal more credit than we deserved for breaking up the Ku Klux Klan. I think the Ku Klux Klan would have been broken up whether we had ever written one word about it or not. I think that if we served any purpose, it was focusing attention in bigger towns and bigger communities than we had on the problem with the Klan and that it drew the FBI and State Bureau of Investigation--that we drew these detectives and undercover agents in this area. They discovered who the members were promoting these floggings quicker than if we hadn't said anything about it. I think it served to kind of prod them into some kind of action, but I have never believed, and I don't believe now, that we deserve as much credit as has been given for breaking up the Ku Klux Klan.

Question: How did the FBI get into the picture? Was it because of the interstate aspect?

Carter: That's the only basis that they could get in. The fact that we were on the state line and some people had been taken out of their homes in one state and flogged across the line in another state made it a federal offense because they had been transported across the line.

Question: You were doing all the reporting and all the editing?

Carter: Yes, I was all one and the same. I was actually making the front page up. I actually made that up myself for eighteen or twenty years. Not only did I write it but when it came off the linotype machine, I set the heads and got it ready to go on the press....

Question: Did you ever during this period come to the point where you felt maybe you ought to drop your crusading against the Klan?

Carter: Not only against the Klan but against a whole lot of other campaigns. I've come to that conclusion. Many times it's a discouraging kind of thing. You go on, you know, for months and months and you live under this tension and this suspense and the threats of violence to you and your family and get to be kind of a nervous wreck...you begin to wonder if it was worth it to begin with.... I have reached the point a lot of times, and I know Lucille, my wife, will agree, that I'd say that the papers that get along the best in this country are the ones that never say anything and I've thought a lot of times that the weekly newspapers where they just report the women's club meetings and the garden clubs and the bridge affairs, they don't have any problems in making a living. But those that really say something, you know, they are putting their future on the line every week...many times I've faced that situation, not just with the Klan campaign, but with some much more risky and dangerous than the Klan. I've faced this situation many times. I've had at least a dozen campaigns as dangerous or moreso than the Ku Klux Klan.

Question: With what issues?

Carter: Well, with corruption and graft among the 13 members of the sheriff's department, for instance, in which I had 38 affidavits from bootleggers and liquor peddlers and gamblers that they were paying off the sheriff's deputies to the extent of several hundred thousand dollars a year in the Myrtle Beach, Horry County area. I lost the case. I lost the fight. I carried it on for 18 months. I was harassed every way you can be harassed. I even had to go before the grand jury with two armed guards that the government sent with me, two federal agents. We knew what we said was the truth and we finally got an FBI case against them for violating the civil rights of people. Never could get the case against them on the bribery and corruption, but we did get a case against all 13 for violating the civil rights of a group of blacks in our community and they were tried in federal court in Florence, South Carolina. This was after I won the Pulitzer prize. We lost the case. The jury found them not guilty. Today, all of them would have been convicted. You couldn't hardly convict them though, 20 years ago. We lost the case in Florence, South Carolina but...I'm not sorry we fought that crusade. Every deputy lost his job. We got a new set of county policemen that did away with the sheriff's department. The legislature passed a law that created a Horry County rural police force and we've never had that problem since...that was one of the most difficult crusades that we were ever involved in.

Carter: We have also been involved in crusades against political machinery in our own county. We used to have some of the crookedest elections in the world in this county. I think we have very fair elections now. But they were crooked because nobody seemed to care. Nobody talked about it and we fought the crooked elections and got the state board of elections to hold various hearings in our county as a result of the things we campaigned against. We fought this with the board of elections in our county numerous times and even when we got the state board of elections to come down and hold hearings on our charges of corruption, they would almost always whitewash them, but it kept calling to the attention of the people the fact that something was going on. I think today we've got clean elections and I think we had a little...part to play in it.

Question: What else do you remember about the Klan?

Carter: I went to Klan public meetings with fear. I guess fortunately all Klan public meetings were held right out in an open field. They would rent some land from a farmer and they would go out and set this truck up and this cross...it was pretty dark and that could be an advantage or a disadvantage. I could hide pretty well in the crowd but I could have easily gotten stabbed or shot in the crowd. I never went alone...I always took somebody. Usually it was one of the printers....

Question: What did you feel? Was it a feeling of revulsion at these people or did you feel a certain sympathy for some of the ideas they expressed?

Carter: I agreed with them on some of the things that they said. I agreed with them on communism, for instance, because I'm about as anti-communist as you can get. I don't want any part of it and I have to say that the Klan didn't want any part of it either. Revulsion? I don't know whether I can say...that exactly. If you hear some people who are not very intelligent to begin with stand up on trucks and just lambast everything in the country, while they may have the right to do that, you can't help but feel some objection to it being said so violently over and over to so many people, and maybe revulsion might have been correct in that instance. But I would go to those meetings. I would make notes of what they said and I'd come back and I'd try to analyze what they had said, and I just didn't want any part of this kind of criticism of our country. I'm not sure that a lot of the things that the Klan said then, if they had said them at some later date in history, might not have been accepted better than in '49, '50, and '51 because there was the time in the '60s when you could just about say anything about the establishment and get a following. So, I'm not too sure that they weren't before their time, that if they had been active during the era of the burnings and demonstrations and other violence that swept the country, they might have gotten more of a foothold than they did and they might have gotten it through a higher caliber of people. Not many of the higher echelon of education got involved with the Klan in the period I'm talking about, but you know if they had gone along with the same anti-establishment things 15 years later, they might have gotten a different following.... Some of the violence that went on in the '60s, while the people involved might have sincerely felt that they were justified, that didn't make it right insofar as I am concerned. I felt like they were breaking the law then. It was just as illegal as the Klan was. I think if it is against the law, it's against the law, and though not all of the laws are right, I think we should be able to change those without breaking them.

Question: Was the revulsion you felt then for the appeal to people's baser emotions rather than to their reason or intellect?

Carter: I spoke of it constantly in the paper as rabble rousing. The hierarchy, the Grand Dragon, the Grand Cyclops, the Imperial Wizard, they had all these fancy names for the officers. They, I think, were involved with it because of the money. The average layman in their group was there because of this adventure thing. He was looking for something other than working ten hours on the farm and going home and going to bed. You see they started their recruiting campaign with a motorcade through your town. They would have a red...lighted cross on the lead car, and there would be 40 or 50 cars in the motorcade. These motorcades would come into your town...and usually go through the colored section. They'd pass out application blanks for members, a printed form. We ran these printed forms in the paper at various times so people would know what they were. We tried to place some of our friends in the Klan with those membership blanks but we could never get one in. We had to get our information from relatives of members or else through the FBI. But most of their public meetings and their motorcades were for the purpose of recruiting and that's how they got the 1500 members in Columbus County and 3500 members in Horry County. You know you haven't asked this but it might cross your mind, how did they get these people out of their homes to beat them up? Well, they were pretty shrewd in that thing. They never went to anybody's house with robes and hoods on and knocked on the door and when they came to the door grabbed them and ran with them. It wasn't ever like that. A total stranger would come to your door and he'd knock on the door and say he was out of gas a half mile down the road or he'd got a sick child in the next block or somebody's dog was run over. Once they got you out of the house, this guy disappears and now the boys with the robes and the hoods, they take you forcibly and go on to the floggings and the beatings. They always got you out of the house with some ruse that you show some compassion for somebody else. There's one other thing I want to point out to you. They were smart enough that when they would have these parades through Tabor City for instance, they didn't use the local members of the Klan in those motorcades because this would have been too easy to pin down. I mean John Doe knows that Sam Brown wasn't home that night, where was he? You see everybody knows where everybody is in a town of 2,000 people. If they were going to have a parade and motorcade in Tabor City, those Klansmen would probably come from Columbia or Spartenburg or Charleston, several hundred miles away.... They would always use outsiders for this kind of motorcade, which I thought this was pretty smart of them.

Question: On the Klan, what specific reporting techniques did you use?

Carter: A whole lot of this kind of reporting is a mixture of news and editorials all in the same paragraphs. You know, I'm sure that they still teach just who, what, when and where and no personal pronouns in the news reporting. Well you couldn't campaign against the Klan on that basis. You had to put your thoughts and analysis and recommendations into the news that you were writing. So, you know, we just used a combination of a little news, what little we could get a hold of, and editorialized it in the news column. We wrote editorials, too, but there's no getting around it, we probably used very poor professional techniques crusading against the Klan but we said what was on our mind, you know, whether it was strictly objective or not; we said what was on our minds and we would still do it today if we were involved with a serious campaign.

WRITING SAMPLES:

CARTER

MASKED MEN BEAT UP TWO COLUMBUS COUNTY CITIZENS

(News Story)

Masked night-riding mobsters enticed a Columbus County resident from his home and then severely beat him in the New Hope section about ten miles from Tabor City last Thursday night, the sheriff's department announced this week.

At the same time, the sheriff disclosed an almost identical flogging that occurred in the Olympic section late last month. No mention of this earlier episode had been disclosed until this week.

The latest victim was Clayton Sellers, 28-year-old married man of the New Hope section, six miles southwest of Whiteville, who was severely beaten about midnight Thursday.

The other case which came to light was that of Robert Lee Gore, who lives in the Olympic section near the South Carolina line.

Sheriff H. Hugh Nance said evidence indicated that Gore was seized by masked men on the last Friday night in October and taken across the state line in Horry County, South Carolina, where he was whipped.

Neither incident was reported immediately, and the known facts in the Gore flogging were turned over the Federal Bureau of Investigation because the victim was carried across the state line. State Bureau of Investigation agents were called into the Sellers case.

Sellers told a press representative, in the presence of Sheriff H. Hugh Nance, that two unmasked men aroused him from sleep about 11 o'clock Thursday night and asked him to let them have some gasoline, claiming their car had run out of fuel.

According to his story, he was engaged in drawing gasoline from his car when another automobile pulled up and stopped. He was seized, but was not loaded into a car until his mother had tried to tear the mask from one of the men and his wife had fired five shots in the direction of his captors.

The victim said he. was taken blindfolded to an "out-of-the-way" spot and beaten with what seemed to be either a piece of machine belt or a piece cut from an automobile tire. Two men beat him alternately on either thigh while two other men held his arms.

He said they gave as an excuse that he had beaten his mother the previous Sunday. He denied to them and to the sheriff that he had ever struck his mother.

22

Sellers exhibited dark spots about eight inches above the knees where he was bruised in the assault.

Following the beating, Sellers said the masked men carried him to a spot about a mile from his home and told him to get out of the car. He said they held a gun on his back and ordered him to "get gone" and not look back. He said several cars were in the procession.

To the sheriff and the newsman, Sellers denied he had ever beaten his mother but admitted that sometime back he had had trouble with his wife. He said, however, they were now living together amicably and that his wife tried to defend him when he was seized.

The Gore flogging, so far as could be learned locally, was similar in detail to the Sellers incident. In that case the victim was also visited about 11 o'clock at night and was persuaded to help two men who claimed their automobile had broken down. He was in the act of getting his car tools to go to their aid when he was grabbed and blindfolded.

According to the information turned over to the FBI, Gore was carried into South Carolina, forced to bend over forward while his captors whipped him with heavy instruments such as described by Sellers.

Sheriff Nance said his officers and Horace L. Shaw, Superintendent of the Columbus County Bureau of Investigation, were working with the SBI and FBI on the two cases, but that he was unable to report any progress at this time.

November 21, 1950

W. Horance Carter

OUR DEFENSE

(Front Page Editorial)

Dear Mr. Hamilton:

Thank you for your letter of January 21, even though most of your remarks are highly slanderous and untrue. However, in at least one respect we see eye-to-eye - we both believe in the freedom of the press and for that reason your letter is printed in this "trash sheet" word for word. I know then that you would have no objection to my offering a few remarks in my defense. Even criminals tried in legal courts have that privilege.

In your first paragraph you repeat a charge made by you months ago that my "mind is warped." Mr. Hamilton, just to deny this statement is not evidence enough, when you consider the source from which the charge came. But perhaps you will accept my challenge to appear with me before any qualified psychiatrist and let him thoroughly examine us both. It might be interesting to see just whose mind is warped. Matter of fact, I believe it would be a revelation.

You insinuate in your first paragraph that my advertisers in the Tribune, as well as subscribers, are affiliated with your organization. Of course, we can neither say you are right or that you are wrong. But we will make this statement. If there are any KKK members advertising with us who would like to cease doing so, we will by happy to cancel it forthwith. If there are any subscribers who would like to have their subscription money refunded, we will refund in cash the remainder of their paid-up subscription time. We ask for no assistance from the Ku Klux Klan. There are enough other people for us to make a living.

In your second paragraph you "are led to challenge" me to prove that your KKKs have had anything to do with the recent Columbus County floggings. Mr. Hamilton, please take note that the column to which you have taken such violent objection stated, "This fear is an outgrowth of the KKK and an evil thereof whether they are the guilty parties in the numerous Columbus County floggings or not."

The coming of your Klan marked the beginning of these floggings and even if your group isn't doing the job themselves, others are using the organization for a haven. But believe me, if I could prove that the KKKs are responsible for just one of them, I would be most happy to tell a jury of twelve men all about it. The group carrying out these floggings gives the defendant no chance to testify for himself. Men are being beaten on the theory that they are guilty without any right to plead innocent.

Your boys will seek legal counsel and a chance to plead their cases when the time necessitates such action. And that's as it should be - innocent until proven guilty.

Then, Mr. Hamilton, there is no difficulty in proving your statement wrong when you said, "I challenge any one to prove where the organization has in any way tried to administer justice to any one." By your own admission, you and your robed friends dragged Charlie Fitzgerald from his place of business in Myrtle Beach and made some violent attempts at your form of administering justice. Did you or didn't you?

And then the constitutional principles to which you refer. Have you ever read that document? A man who so roundly criticizes the law, the Negro, the Jew, the Catholics in public speeches everywhere and who still professes to believe in the principles of our democratic government is stretching an interpretation much further than I can imagine.

You have asked what was wrong with the law officers of Columbus County. As to their ability to track down these criminals, who have made one assault after another, I do not know. As to their efforts in this direction, I am confident they have done their best. Pitted against such an undercover policy society perhaps makes it too big a job for them.

But at any rate they are lending their assistance to a big brother, the FBI, along with the SBI (State Bureau of Investigation), from whom they have every right to request help, and it is our belief that they are making progress, and that there is no reason to believe there is anything wrong with our law enforcement.

Should they fail miserably to hang one of these crimes on the proper persons, then I will have to agree with you that there's some ability or something lacking. I do not minimize their task. It's difficult to procure the evidence. With that, they have my sympathies and best wishes.

As to the caliber of men in your Klan, I can only say "no comment." But I would like to have the membership roster held up before God to get His stamp of approval on a group of hand-picked righteous people who can hide their identity and their faces and do no wrong.

In your last two paragraphs you get back to God and Country, both dear to my heart, and to which I can only say "amen." But as to the missions given by God, I can't help but wonder if God gave you your mission, or if He gave me mine. Or if He had rather you cease your operation or me mine.

Very sincerely yours,

W. Horace Carter

January 23, 1952

KLAN KING ARRESTED; CONSPIRACY CHARGED

(News Story - Condensed)

Thomas L. Hamilton, "Imperial Wizard" of the Ku Klux Klan in the Carolinas, returned to Columbus County Monday through the persuasive powers of the law.

In sharp contrast to the 5,000 persons who attended his initial Klan rally last August, less then 35 people were on hand to catch a glimpse of him as he appeared at the courthouse about 10:30 o'clock to accept service on warrants charging him with conspiracy to kidnap and conspiracy to assault in connection with two Columbus floggings.

Dressed in a natty navy blue suit, Hamilton made bond of $5,000 in each of the two cases. The bonds were signed by Mrs. Roger Bullock of Fair Bluff who lives in the Spring Branch section of Horry County.

The former "Grand Dragon," who promoted himself to "Imperial Wizard" following the Klan invasion of this county last year, is scheduled to appear in Recorder's Court on June 10.

Hamilton, accompanied by one of his lawyers, Waldo Hyman of Florence, had nothing to say during his brief sojourn in Whiteville. He shook hands with a couple of county officials but made no comment pertinent to the charges for which he was arrested Saturday.

Unrobed and without any white-robed "Imperial Guard," Hamilton looked like an average, unspectacular businessman.

The 44-year old Hamilton, plump and bespectacled, surrendered in the office of his lawyer in Florence, S.C. about 2:30 o'clock Saturday afternoon, some 20 hours after warrants had been sworn out against him by North Carolina officers.

The surrender was made several hours after George Keels of Florence revealed that the Klan chieftain would give himself up at that point.

The ex-grocer posted $10,000 immediately after his arrest and left immediately in a friend's car and refused to tell newsmen where he was going.

Hamilton waived extradition and agreed to appear here this morning to post the appearance bond....

State Bureau of Investigation agents took the warrants to Columbia on Friday. A fugitive warrant was signed at Lexington and the hunt for Hamilton was on. But he had left his home at Leesville when officers went there to arrest him....

Solicitor Clifton L. Moore of Burgaw prepared his warrants several days before they were to be served on Hamilton. One warrant charges the

KKK chieftain was a conspirator in the flogging of Evergreen Flowers, a Negro woman who lives near Chadbourn and who was beaten with sticks on the night of January 18, 1951.

"We didn't know there was a Klansman within miles," at the time of that flogging, Solicitor Moore said. Gradually as the evidence unravelled, it became apparent that the downfall of the North Carolina branch of the Klan could be traced to the beating of the Flowers woman.

She was beaten by a mob "of 40 or 50 men" and was struck once with the butt of a gun. Her husband was believed to have been the intended victim but he escaped by fleeing out a back door.

The Flowers family moved to Cerro Gordo after the incident. The tenant home they occupied was destroyed by fire 33 days later and the origin of the fire remains a mystery.

Solicitor Moore also linked Hamilton with the flogging of Woodrow Jackson, the Whiteville mechanic, who was beaten in a cemetery for excessive drinking. And the solicitor intimated strongly he may be able to connect the Grand Dragon with at least one other flogging case, in the role of conspirator....

Charged with conspiracy to incite to mob violence in Horry County in 1950, he escaped trial when the grand jury refused to return indictments against him and several of his Klan associates.

This case grew out of a Myrtle Beach demonstration by the Klan at a Negro night club. A Conway policeman in the traditional robe of the Klan was slain in an exchange of gunfire.

The Klan's "Imperial Wizard" also faced a similar charge two years ago at Camden after a YMCA worker at Sumter was beaten by the Klan.

A Federal grand jury indicted Hamilton last June for violating the postal laws after he had been accused of mailing a postal card containing statements "obviously intended to reflect injuriously upon the character and conduct" of Wilton E. Hall, a newspaper publisher at Anderson.

To escape a prison term of one year, Hamilton chose to pay a $1,000 fine.

Since the first flogging began in Columbus County late last year, officers had been anxious to grab Hamilton. They got their chance after several admitted Klansmen were put on the witness stands in Whiteville and Wilmington, and after the KKK members had been grilled privately by State and Federal investigators.

Rev. Connor, a 50-year-old farmer of Cerro Gordo, Route 1, who pleaded no contest to charges that he helped flog Woodrow Johnson, Whiteville mechanic, first introduced the name of Hamilton in Columbus Superior Court.

Early Brooks, "Exalted Cyclops" of the Fair Bluff Klavern, read a letter from Hamilton at one of the Klan meetings, Connor remembered. The letter, Connor added, "said that some Fair Bluff women had written him (Hamilton) that a horse trader would have this woman's husband arrested and then go out with her."

Hamilton said "He wanted it taken care of immediately," Connor quoted the letter as saying.

Steve Edmund, the 25-year-old roly poly Columbus farmer who was a star witness for the prosecution in both the State and Federal trials, said he filled out his Klan membership blank "and gave it to Hamilton."

Along with the blank, Edmund said he gave the KKK grand dragon $10 for an initiation fee, $6 for a robe and hood, and $2 for the quarter's dues.

Another link in the evidence against Hamilton was forged by Walter A. Murphy, who is in charge of the Charlotte FBI office. In the Federal trial, Murphy testified that after Early Brooks was arrested, Brooks said Hamilton promised him (Brooks) $4 out of each $10 collected from new Klan members.

"Swayed by Speech"

Like Edmund, another former Klansman, Frank Lewis of Fair Bluff, said he was swayed by Hamilton's vitriolic speech at the first Klan crossburning in Columbus in August, 1951. Lewis, a former Fair Bluff police chief, later repented and helped implicate other Klansmen.

Referring to the cross-burning when Hamilton, surrounded by hooded figures, stood on an improvised platform to deliver his speeches of hate, Lewis said truthfully:

"I wish I took a rock and knocked him (Hamilton) off that stand."

Hamilton always had contended that the only beatings the Klan condoned are those which occur "at the ballot boxes." He had piously proclaimed that "disgruntled persons," non-Klan members, have carried out floggings under the insignia of the Klan.

Early in 1952 after a Methodist minister had been threatened by the Klan and later hospitalized with a nervous condition, Hamilton publicly disbanded the Fair Bluff Klavern for un-Klanish activities....

Hamilton is a former wholesale grocer in Leesville who crossed the North Carolina state line on Klan business at the August, 1951, crossburning. Wearing his black robe and hood, he lambasted the Negroes, Jews, Catholics and Communists while his followers circulated through a crowd of 5,000 with Klan membership blanks.

His sermon of hate proved potent. Slightly more than 1,500 citizens of Columbus County were Klansmen less than four months later. Just across the line in Horry County, S.C., there are an estimated 3,000 to 5,000 dues-paying KKK members.

Klansmen who took the witness stands at the two trials had not the slightest idea about the destination of their initiation fees and dues. Presumbly, most of it went to Hamilton, who had said his considerable treasury uses the money to help charitable causes. Those causes were not identified....

May 28, 1952

(Story condensed slightly)

W. Horance Carter

You don't count costs...you become involved.

CARO BROWN
Alice (Tex.) Echo
Pulitzer Prize—Public Service
1955

3

In the arid flatlands of South Texas, Duval County and neighboring Jim Wells County were known for decades as the political fiefdom of the Parr family. The Parrs were Spanish-speaking Anglos who represented the last of a vanishing breed in Texas politics: "Patrons" or "bosses" who gave help and guidance to Mexican-Americans who in return voted as they were instructed.

George B. Parr, called the "Duke of Duval," committed suicide in 1975 after years of delivering a block vote of Mexican-Americans to Parr candidates. His power had been inherited from his father, Archie, a state senator, who had allied himself with Mexican-Americans in a 1912 struggle with Anglo leaders over political control of Duval County.

In 1948 George Parr came to national attention when Jim Wells County produced just enough votes for Lyndon B. Johnson to give him an 87-vote margin statewide in the race for the U.S. Senate that launched Johnson on the road to the White House. Numerous allegations of fraud were made involving Parr, but the disputed election was upheld in a court battle.

In the late 1940s Parr's empire, guarded by his private army of "gun-toting" henchmen, began to topple. First, the Freedom Party, the first organized resistance to Parr's control in 40 years, was formed in Duval County by Mexican-American World War II veterans and others who charged that the "Duke" had enriched himself at public expense. Second, the administration of Governor Allan Shivers, with whom Parr had a political falling-out, sent Texas Rangers and representatives of the attorney general's office to Duval County to investigate conditions in the spring of 1952. Before their appearance, Parr had himself appointed sheriff, by far the most important office in a South Texas county.

31

The tense atmosphere produced violence and intrigue and led to two murders, one of a radio reporter in 1949, and the other of Jacob Floyd, Jr., the son of an anti-Parr leader, who was killed by mistake during an attempt to murder his father in September, 1952. It also led to a remarkable journalistic feat by a reporter for the Daily Echo of Alice, Texas, county seat of Jim Wells County.

This was Caro Brown, a housewife turned reporter, who doggedly followed the Parr case for nearly three years as fresh scandals, charges, and countercharges unfolded almost daily following the 1952 murder. There were grand jury investigations, court orders restraining officials from destroying records, resignations of county office holders, judges and school board members, court inquiries, hearings, indictments and more indictments. Through it all she got the facts, not only for her own paper with its three-person reporting staff, but also for the Associated Press. The AP relied heavily on Brown's reporting to keep the news media across the nation informed on the Duval County story. For her efforts she won the 1955 Pulitzer prize for local reporting under deadline pressure. She was the fourth women winner of a Pulitzer prize and the first honored for local reporting.

Born in 1908 in Baber, Tex., Brown stumbled into the Parr story by accident. The wife of a civil engineer and mother of three, she moved to Alice in 1947 and started working for the Echo as a $15 a week proofreader after becoming bored with a housewife's routine. As a young woman she had studied journalism at what is now Texas Women's University, but she had been sent home in disgrace for breaking school rules by attending a dance. Before marriage she had worked as a legal secretary and had learned shorthand. Since she had lived in Cuba with her family as a child, she was fluent in Spanish. Both Spanish and shorthand helped her in her prize-winning reporting.

Assigned to the Parr story the night of the Floyd murder, she stayed with it in spite of personal danger, tragedy, and little support from her own newspaper. The Texas Rangers warned her that her life might be in danger from Parr forces that did not want their activities publicized. They told her to carry a gun on lonely drives from Duval County to Alice after late-night court hearings. Once she stood in a courthouse hallway and personally broke up a brawl between Parr and a captain of the Texas Rangers, writing a first-person story about it.

In 1953 her youngest child drowned in a swimming pool accident, but still she kept on with the story. "I stayed away from work five days and I felt the best thing to do was to get back," she said. Her paper never paid her more than $50 a week - $15 less than the sports reporter - and did not even cover her expenses. She quit the week she won the Pulitzer and did not continue in journalism except for a brief return to the Echo. Now a widow, she lives in Corpus Christi, Tex.

BROWN INTERVIEW

Question: During the years when you reported on the Duval situation, how dependent were the reporters for the establishment press, the big papers and the AP on your work?

Brown: Well, naturally, I covered it day-by-day and they would follow my work on AP. But, when they would come into the area they would always touch base with me, you know. I liked to give them the local color because it was one of a kind, this area, and it was so unbelievable that I knew they wouldn't have time to pick up these little stories that would give color to their work...and...add interest. It isn't just a dull courtroom procedure when you can dwell on little incidents that happened or the characters.

Question: You must have spent hours then filling in the visiting reporters?

Brown: Yes, but I enjoyed it as much as they did. I always looked forward to it and I learned so .much from them. I love to watch the pros work. They taught me a lot.

Question: What did they teach you specifically?

Brown: Well, ...I would read their stories and I learned how they handled their work, how they handled their stories,...just routine

33

reporting was new to me because I had never been taught courtroom work or anything like that, and they, lots of them, were versed in courtroom procedure.

Brown: They were experienced...most of them came from cities and most of them specialized in that type of work or some just did general reporting, but there were some real sharp--all men, there were no women.

Question: Did you ever feel a victim of sex discrimination as a woman reporter?

Brown: Not in covering that story, no, and in fact I don't think it mattered. It was wonderful, the attitude that educated professional men in the legal profession and judges had (toward women) and I knew they liked publicity and I didn't color it (the story) and I think maybe they shaped up because of it. I don't know. Maybe at times it helped...to know that this story was going to be sent all over the country....

Question: Of all the stories that you wrote, what would you estimate was the average amount of time you spent per story?

Brown: Well, when you ask that question, I have to say that you don't count just the time that you're at the typewriter. My whole day started early and very often I would sit and take my notes through a very harried session in the morning over there at court. Sometimes there would be more than one action. In other words, there would be a grand jury session and then the court session and I would go out during recess and call AP and come back at noon and get out my story. Of course, we ran a story the morning after. We had an afternoon paper and we would pick up the story of the day before but then...I would call in to AP usually at noon if there was something happening that they needed at that time. Then I would sort of start my story and I would go in a grocery story and get a piece of cheese and a few crackers and put them in the seat of the car and go back to court, which sometimes lasted until four or five o'clock. Then I would come back and I would have to write my story. I know I was exhausted but at that time that was it.... Sometimes there would be two and three stories that had to be written and I would have to edit them myself because I was the only one there. I would have to go back over them, clean them up and have them ready for the next morning.

Question: Was your background in Spanish useful?

Brown: Oh wonderful, wonderful. I don't know how I could have survived without it. It helped a lot and also I loved the sense of humor of the people and the language is very colorful and I honestly enjoyed a lot of little jokes. They would come and tell me the little jokes, you know, that they would share among themselves and I enjoyed that.

Question: And you had been a legal secretary, so you knew shorthand?

Brown: Yes, without planning anything, all these things worked together fortunately in my work. They worked to help me and...I couldn't have survived without a combination like that because things happened too fast....

Question: You seemed to have an incredible combination of skills and background that helped you?

Brown: Yes, just luck. Yes, it did, and I hadn't thought about it in just precisely those terms but that's so right. In spite of the fact that I hadn't worked at journalism, hadn't completed my education in it, and hadn't thought seriously of ever getting into it, and then to be dropped into it over my head. All the things combined to help me and in life you don't know what experience will help you. But you know in advising young people who are studying journalism, I can't stress too much a general education because for each interview you have, you need to know something about the questions you should ask a person and that is when you realize your ignorance, so the more that you can prepare ahead of time, the more qualified you are and the more at ease you will be because you're going to have to prepare anyway. You have more self-confidence if you are informed on a subject.... I can't stress that too much.

Question: How did you get informed on the background of the Duval situation when you started working on the paper? Did the editor tell you or did you just keep your ears open?

Brown: It was a quick education. I had to go to anybody who had lived here a long time and had been interested in it (the story) and kept up with it. There were a number and they were only too glad to tell the story and little by little the blocks fell into place, but there's always one that's been missing. I wish I knew the whole story. I still don't know it. I don't think it will ever be clear.

Question: The extent of the corruption?

Brown: Yes.

Question: And the entrenchment of the machine?

Brown: Yes, and the answers to so many mysteries that have come up. You know we've had murders that haven't been solved and so many things. They have a way of burying their secrets.

Question: I'm sure that your job meant a lot more to you than the paycheck you got. How much did you make?

Brown: The most I ever made was $50 a week ($15 less than the sports reporter).

Question: Did you get a raise when you won the Pulitzer Prize?

Brown: No.

Question: Obviously, it wasn't a nine-to-five job and obviously it wasn't a job that paid well.... Why were you willing to put so much of yourself into it?

Brown: I've wondered about that myself because what I did in some ways came very near wrecking my health and there were lots of heartbreaking things during those days. But I think involvement--you don't count costs at the time - you become involved. There was no point that I thought I could drop it, and actually this is unbelievable and probably if I had had to live just totally on that tiny salary, I might have gotten out and gotten a nine-to-five job and hated it. But this meant enough to me, and there was nothing in the world that could have made me drop the story and I often footed my bills when I would leave town to cover a case. My expenses weren't all paid even but I was so involved it meant enough to me personally to do that job and do it to the finish. And when I won the award I felt that I had done my job. At that point the activity had slowed down and I felt that I had done my job and I resigned.

Question: Did you feel in doing your job that you were representing the public's right to know what was going on?

Brown: I certainly did. At times I would be just furious at attempts to keep me from getting the facts...they made every attempt in the world to keep the records from the press, and it wasn't until late in the case that you had any right to just demand that they open the records to you.

Question: You speak of "they," you mean the powerful political machine?

Brown: Yes, any of the officials, county officials in charge of records. We would know the records were there. We would know that a certain thing had happened and was in the records but there was a cynical attitude and you knew they were laughing at you when you would go in and ask, and they would make some silly excuse such as they couldn't find it or they thought they had loaned it to another official and he hadn't returned it and such silly things as that.

Question: Did you fear for your life?

Brown: I was aware there was danger any time you went in there (Duval County). They were a law unto themselves. It was evident that they were desperate. They knew that their backs were to the wall and you know, with human nature you can't say what will happen next and we were all aware of that, all investigators.... I was making waves.

Question: What did it feel like the first time you crossed that border from Jim Wells County where Alice, a comparatively safe town, is located and went into Duval County?

Brown: I'm going to tell you about the first time I went when it was a frightening thing. This was when an investigative reporter had come in very furtively, contacting an informer who had gotten hold of some records and was...letting him have access to these records. This reporter was called before the grand jury and he...begged me to go with him because reporters didn't like to go in alone. I didn't go with him because I was covering another case, but I promised him I would come later.

Question: This was a Parr grand jury?

Brown: A Parr grand jury.

Question: In other words, a grand jury that was trying to hush up the whole mess?

Brown: Hush it up and get rid of anybody who was giving them any trouble.

Question: Including possibly a reporter?

Brown: Yes. This man was writing a series for his paper in Houston...when I got there it was dusk and this session was on in this bleak little court house--dim lights in the hallway--so I...went in and an armed deputy was at the top of the stairs guarding the grand jury and this reporter opened the door from the courtroom next door and his face was ashen...he whispered to this deputy asking him if he could talk to me and the deputy consented and I went up the stairs and he pulled me into this courtroom and he whispered to me, he said, "Caro, don't leave. Stay around," he says, "Diego (who was the informer) is spilling his guts and I don't know what they will do to me." He said, "I figure I will be next... I want to give you three names and if I'm not out in a reasonable time I want you to phone these three men in the order I have written."

Question: Had Diego been a member of the gang and then become an informer and now he was talking to the gang again?

Brown: Yes. I believe so. Well, he was talking because he was scared to death. Diego had been, I believe, some minor official in the system and he had managed to get hold of these records.... I told (the reporter) I wouldn't leave until he came out and as though it had been a prepared script, at that moment the attorney general's man, who had been undercover, walked up the stairs with his briefcase under his arm and knocked on the door and showed his credentials and for the first time an official was allowed into a Parr grand jury and after that, the tension went out, and I returned home. But I saw a very, very terrified man.

Question: So you started covering the story when a young man was killed by accident by a Parr-hired thug who was trying to get the man's father since he was the leader of a reform political party?

Brown: Yes.

Question: And then because you were sent to the hospital where the young man was taken, you just continued with the story?

Brown: Yes. There was only an editor and me and a sports reporter at that time...and it was my story. The editor couldn't leave his post and it was just understood that I would cover it and it immediately went into court proceedings and it was a day-by-day thing. So it was my story and it was a frightening thing because I had never had anything of that type to cover and it was certainly new to me, but I somehow managed. I think you do under stress. That's a reporter's problem. You don't have your stories planned out for you. They don't happen that way. If you're just a general reporter, you don't know what's going to happen...that's the reason I say get your general education and learn to get along with people and get some self-confidence and then play it by ear. Just stay in there.

Question: You have to tell it like it is?

Brown: Yes, yes. That's the only way.

Question: What about the personal abuse that you took and the gossip that was spread about you?

Brown: Oh, that goes with the territory. I would hear those things...because what they were trying to do was cut me down.... There was nothing personal,... I was a threat to them because they didn't want this thing emblazoned over the front pages of the state papers. They would have loved to kept it in their pocket but it (gossip) really didn't bother me.... I knew that the people knew the situation understood and it didn't bother me.

Question: Is there any one thing that stands out most in your mind about those stories that you wrote? Any one principle of journalism?

Brown: I don't know how long I would have stayed in journalism or how hard I would have worked if I hadn't become so personally involved and interested. I don't know how I could work on a paper unless the stories I wrote meant something to me...the only type of journalism that I like or that I would ever do again would be the type where I could choose my stories.

Question: So you feel that journalism must be a personal commitment?

Brown: I think it is, or a person should get out. I can't imagine a hack thing of just going and just writing. That type of thing. Yes, I think you've got to love the work and to me there's nothing more beautiful than being with a group of newspaper people. There's nothing dull; there's no boredom. You don't wonder if somebody catches your innuendos, you know. Everybody is alert there, half cynical, and they have know-how and it's fun talking to people in the trade. I love it.

Brown: Writing the story--that's hard. I use to worry about my lead because the idea then was to grab the attention of the fellow who is drinking coffee and on his way to work or something. Get his attention, let him skim through it and usually when I was getting my material together--when I was taking down my story, or as I was driving back to work, I would be planning the lead.... But, it isn't easy. I remember, my AP state editor and I went across the street from the court house to George Parr's office and George came to the door and we stood and talked to him about the case...it was evidently at a hot time or the AP man wouldn't have been here and so he files his story when we get back to the hotel and he comes back with a grin from ear to ear. "Caro," he quoted the lead to me, "George Parr stood in the sun." He was so proud of that lead, he was like a new reporter who has passed muster.

Brown: A writer's vocabulary should be No. 1.   Without it, he's like a soldier without a weapon.   He hasn't got anything to work with....   He has got to learn those words.   He's got to love them.   He's got to feel them and roll them off his tongue.   Try them--some words are beautiful, some express just the opposite.   It is absolutely beautiful when the English language can be used to its fullest and that's a must.   That isn't something you should do, it's something you MUST do, or you're lost.   You're just gonna be a hack.

WRITING SAMPLES:

BROWN

RANGERS ASSURE SECRET BALLOT BY DESTROYING VOTE

(News Story)

Duval county voters were given concrete evidence here today of the secret ballot in the last election when impounded ballots and stubs from that county were burned under orders of District Judge Sam G. Reams.

Acting in accordance with the order, Texas Rangers, led by Captain Alfred Allee, first visited the office of Tax Assessor-Collector Jack Gladney in Alice, where the 39 ballot boxes, impounded under court order on August 26th, were turned over to them.

Later, the group, made up of Allee, Joe Bridge and Wiley Williamson, went to the office of District Clerk Bub Carlisle, where they were given the 12 stub boxes.

The Rangers, assisted by workers in the courthouse, then loaded the boxes onto a pickup truck. Captain Allee took the wheel, while Wiley Williamson perched precariously atop the metal boxes in the rear of the truck.

Went to Courthouse

Upon their arrival here at 11:50 a.m., the group went immediately to the county courthouse. Upon finding that the county clerk, J.G. Perez, had left the courthouse for the day, the Rangers made inquiries and later found Perez at the Tortilla Shop, while Garcia was located at the A&M Bar.

The two were presented the paper which ordered them to burn the stubs and ballots and other election materials in the presence of the Rangers. They were then told to meet the Rangers at the courthouse at 1 p.m. and to then proceed with the destruction of the controversial ballots and stubs.

After discussing suitable places for the burning, a ravine within a few hundred yards of the El Ranchito nignt club was selected.

Stopping long enough to buy a large can of kerosene to hasten the burning, the group proceeded to the out-of-the-way spot and began the job which is unprecedented in the political history of Duval county.

Contents Dumped

The stub boxes, sealed by both Perez and by Carlisle, were first opened and their contents dumped on the fire beside the narrow road.

42

Later, Garcia, using keys which he brought along in a sealed packet, and helped by the officers, opened the larger boxes which contained the ballots. The ballots were added to the flames. Upon finding a number of pencils and several bottles of ink in one of the boxes, Ranger Joe Bridge asked, "What do you want me to do with these?"

"The order says to burn everything--burn'em," Allee ordered.

Allee had told Perez earlier that he would be glad to have County Judge Dan Tobin present at the destruction of the ballots, but Perez reported he was unable to reach the judge by phone.

During the latter part of the work, the dry grass surrounding the bonfire became ignited and although the officers managed to keep it under control for a time, it was finally necessary to call the fire department.

Approximately a dozen men answered the call, and remained after putting out the fire to see that it didn't spread again.

No Hard Feelings

A bystander, when told what the Rangers were burning, shrugged his shoulders. "It is much better that way -- now there can be no hard feelings on either side."

Curiously, the incident, significant as it was, failed to attract the crowd as such things ordinarily do. A pick-up truck, with two men inside, approached the group of men as they first began their work. Pausing long enough to take a good look, the driver backed the truck up and returned the way he had come.

Even the sight of the smoke and the sound of the fire siren failed to bring the crowd which usually gathers at a fire. A small group of youngsters straggled up, accompanied by a shaggy dog. From across a deep gulley, a family watched curiously, but made no move to come nearer. Otherwise, the workers worked without spectators.

The Rangers remained at the spot until all the papers were burned, and the charred remains stirred thoroughly to turn up any mark. One said, "Well, I knew Duval county votes were hot, but I never expected they would have to call out the fire department to put out the fire!"

The order for the destruction of the impounded ballots was given in compliance with the new election law. This law provided that 60 days after the date of the election, should no election contest be filed involving the ballots or stubs impounded and should no grand jury indicate a desire of inspecting or examining such ballots or stubs, then they should be destroyed.

September 27, 1953

Caro Brown

AMIABLE CHAT NOT SO AT END

(First-Person News Story)

I've learned never to leave the scene just because things are dull. That's when the lid usually pops off in South Texas.

That's why I stuck around today as Sheriff Archer Parr of Duval county; his uncle, George B. Parr, the South Texas politico, Ranger Capt. Alfred Allee and Ranger Joe Bridge started what was apparently an amiable conversation in the courthouse hall.

The older Parr was here for his hearing on a charge of unlawfully carrying a pistol.

Six Feet Away

I was about six feet away when Ranger Bridge slapped Archer Parr, setting off a chain of action that left spectators shaken long after it was over.

As I watched I could tell that the talk between the sheriff and Bridge was becoming heated and I shushed the man who was talking to me. "Something's fixing to happen," I warned.

Well, I don't appreciate the run-round I got," Bridge told Archer Parr.

Reply Interrupted

"Well, I know of some things you've done unbecoming..." Archer Parr answered. His reply was interrupted by Bridge's fists, which knocked Archer's glasses to the floor.

Faster than we could keep up with it, Bridge struck the younger Parr, knocking the latter's glasses to the floor. George Parr jumped forward at that, and immediately Allee grabbed him, at the same time disarming the sheriff, who had reached for his gun.

(George) Parr's left ear received an open tear when it was twisted by the Ranger captain, who also hit Parr with his fist before sticking his gun in his ribs.

'Please Don't'

At that point I stepped into the middle, begging, "Cap, please don't, please don't."

Repeatedly the Ranger captain told George Parr:

"I've had all I'm going to take off you and the way you've been handling things."

44

He then shoved Parr roughly into the county courtroom; motioned Sheriff Parr to come inside along with Bridge.

"We're going to get this thing settled right here," Allee (said)...

Polishes Glasses

Archer Parr nervously polished his glasses, which had come through the fracas unbroken, while George Parr nodded agreement to what Allee said. At one time the captain said:

"I'm not going to put up with any whipping with pistols or Winchesters in Duval county. Those people have a right to have political meetings without being molested."

Parr nodded, promising that he would not interfere with such meetings.

Later, Archer came to me and said:

"Caro, thanks for doing what you could to stop the trouble."

I said: "Archer, please try to keep things straight-let's not have any more things happen that we'll be sorry for."

"Well, I'll try," Archer Parr replied, "but you know how our tempers get us some times."

January 9, 1954

Caro Brown

PARR HENCHMAN IMPLICATES 'DUKE' IN MISDEEDS

(News Story)

The first open break in the Parr political machine came to light this week when Richard Barton, 44, rancher and former trustee of the Benavides Independent School district, told a Freedom Party gathering, "I was with Parr in stealing money from the school kids."

Barton appeared unexpectedly before more than 2000 people in San Diego (Tex.) Sunday night to answer charges he said Parr leveled at him the previous night at an Old Party rally in Benavides.

"I am ashamed to be here before this crowd because I am trash, a killer and a rat, as George Parr called me last night," Barton told the crowd.

My sisters got together tonight and begged me not to come to this rally because they were afraid Parr would kill me. But I am here, George. If you want to kill me, do it yourself. But don't hire somebody else to do it for you," he challenged, pointing toward the Windmill Cafe where he said he was told Parr was sitting with friends.

As the crowd whooped gleefully at each revelation, Barton went on, "I may be trash, because I was with him in stealing money from school kids."

Referring to the slaying of Luis Reyna, approximately 17 years ago, which he said Parr spoke of the night before, Barton continued, "I am a killer because Dan Garcia, the sheriff, did not help me to avoid the killing. I went twice to see him to get him to straighten things out. He promised me twice he was going to Benavides the next day, but he didn't show up either time."

Without giving more details of the killing, Barton told listeners, "George Parr said last night that when my brother and I were tried for murder he paid for the whole thing."

Again pointing toward the nearby cafe, he asked, "How about that thousand dollars I paid Manuel Raymond and the thousand dollars my brother paid him? And how about the $1500 I paid Quentin Wright?"

Barton referred to M.J. Raymond, Laredo attorney, and Wright, a former San Diego and Alice lawyer.

"The trial went just as George had ordered it," Barton said. "He was first going to send my brother, Jimmie, to the pen. Jimmie was constable and wouldn't do what George ordered, but what he thought was right."

As the audience strained to hear every word, Barton continued. "To get out of trouble and go free, my brother Jimmie had to promise George

46

Parr to resign as constable and get out of the county. George made him resign in front of me and then he made him promise to leave before he would let him go free. Jimmie left the county and has been gone 16 years."

Barton told the exuberant gathering, "I was an Old Party member until this morning. But now I am a Freedom Party member, and I want all the people here to vote for their candidates. From now on I'm going to help win the election."

In an exclusive interview Monday night, Barton said that when the investigation of county and school funds began he planned to sell his property and get out of the county.

"But now I want to stay and help the Freedom Party. I don't intend to leave until they get rid of George Parr and his party," he said flatly. "If he wants to say anything more about me I'm ready to answer him any time, any where."

Barton said he did not attend the Benavides rally, but was told by a relative of the speech Parr made.

The former trustee resigned, along with the three other board members on February 10th, when the school records were impounded by order of the court. He later appeared before the grand jury.

Friday the Duval county grand jury returned indictments against George Parr and 11 other men in connection with charges of a conspiracy to steal property and funds in excess of $50 from the Benavides Independent School district.

Included in the dozen names on the indictments were those of the three men who resigned with Barton shortly after the four turned over the books of the school district for impoundment. They were Jesus Garza, Santiago Garcia and O. Saenz.

The school superintendent, R.W. Mulligan, was also indicted as a member of the conspiracy.

Alice men named in the conspiracy were George Parr's brother, Givens Parr, and B.F. (Tom) Donald, both officials of the Texas State Bank of Alice, former depository of the school funds.

July 20, 1954

Caro Brown

...we had to live within the law.

BUFORD BOONE
Tuscaloosa (Ala.) News
Pulitzer Prize—Editorial Writing
1957

4

The University of Alabama nestles physically and emotionally in the heart of Tuscaloosa, a normally sedate community of 50,000. But in 1956 the tranquillity of the small city was shaken when a black, Autherine Lucy, was admitted to the all-white University.

Her enrollment sparked four days of rioting by segregationists outraged at this token breach of the color line. The vehement opposition caused the administration to bar Lucy on Feb. 6, 1956, despite the fact that federal law supported her, and she never returned.

Amidst the inflammatory rhetoric and angry demonstrations, Buford Boone, publisher of the Tuscaloosa News, called for reason and restraint through the medium of his editorial pages.

Boone himself wrote the editorials related to the Lucy case to avoid charges of non-Southern interference being leveled at his editor who was from New Jersey. Born in Newman, Georgia, in 1909, Boone claims an unquestionable Southern heritage: Great-grandfather and grandfather killed fighting for the South in the Civil War; his father a Georgia state legislator. And from that heritage--commitment to a cause and respect for the law--Boone pressed for law and order despite community criticism, verbal abuse, and threats of violence.

The intensity of emotions is illustrated by the following incident. Nearly a year after the riot Boone spoke to an irate White Citizens Council whose members suggested that he be thrown out the window, and shouts of "kill him," and "hang him" thickened the air.

49

Boone was awarded the Pulitzer Prize for Editorial Writing in 1957 for "his fearless and reasoned editorials in a community inflamed by a segregation issue." In 1958, he himself was a member of the Pulitzer jury.

In addition, he won the George Washington medal for editorial writing from the Freedoms Foundation and awards from Colby College and the University of Alabama for his stand against mob rule.

A graduate of Mercer College, Macon, Georgia, Boone rose from being a reporter to editor of the Macon Telegraph and News. During World War II he was a special agent of the Federal Bureau of Investigation. From 1947 to 1968 he was the publisher of the Tuscaloosa News. A former president of the Tuscaloosa Hotel Co., Boone also was active in Boy Scout and YMCA campaigns.

In the following interview Boone, now retired, reflects on this painful period from a journalist's perspective of history. The parents of a son and a daughter, he and his wife Frances still live in Tuscaloosa among old friends and aging enemies. If Boone harbors any resentment it doesn't show, and his affection for his community and his optimism for the South are evident.

BOONE INTERVIEW

Question: What happened in Tuscaloosa after 1954 when the Supreme Court ruled that desegregation of schools should take place?

Boone: It all started with Autherine Lucy. We had editorials before then. We were one of the few newspapers in the Southeast that supported Eisenhower's decision to go into Little Rock...but the Lucy situation was what triggered the whole thing (here).

Question: What were the other papers in the South doing regarding racial news?

Boone: They were printing news on the front pages that occurred in Tuscaloosa and burying it if it occured in their own hometown. Birmingham did not discover the story it had with reference to racial difficulties until it ended up with the bombing of a church. Birmingham had a story on the front page about some racial difficulties in Macon, Ga, and the Birmingham stuff was on the inside page; the Macon paper had a front page story on what was going on in Birmingham and what was going on in their own town was on the inside.

Question: Did you take any position prior to the actual day when Miss Lucy was escorted to campus by police?

Boone: I don't remember, but I don't think so. We were consistent all along in taking the position that, number one, we had to abide by the court decision whether we liked it or not and number two, we

51

had to live within the law. We had to be governed by the laws of the country. Those were our two primary and consistent positions.

Question: But you do not see yourself as an integrationist?

Boone: No. I knew that it was coming and I knew that we had to accept it, and I was ready to accept it, but I was not promoting it.

Question: Was the community opposition intense to any black coming to the University of Alabama?

Boone: Absolutely. Not only against blacks, but there was great resentment against us because our editorials referred to the group out there as a "mob." There was great, great resentment. We had nice cultured ladies who said that this girl (Lucy) ought to be dragged through the streets of Tuscaloosa. My lawyer...said that he thought the editorials would end up winning some very fine awards but he thought it was a grave error to have run them. That was typical of the community scene.

Question: The community did not foresee that integration was inevitable?

Boone: Oh no, we had a great many people who were ready to start fighting again over it and I'm serious. A great many people were ready to start the Civil War again.... The relationship here is extremely good between the University and a University-level group in the community, but Tuscaloosa also has a large population that, for want of a better word, I will call rednecks and the relationship between them and the University is not too good.

Question: When you came out and called for the community to uphold the court orders...what was the attitude of your other staff members?

Boone: Well, I was the boss and they kept their mouths shut.

Question: At the time that the Lucy episode occurred, how large was the City of Tuscaloosa?

Boone: It was about 50,000, I'd say.

Question: What percentage of blacks?

Boone: About 30 percent.

Question: So obviously since the white feeling was so strong against the admission of Autherine Lucy to the University...the community must have been ready to blow up?

Boone: The sale of firearms and ammunition here shot sky high among blacks and whites. It was not unusual for a person to go to collect a bill and have a person come to the door with a gun in his hand. And what worried me so very, very much was the possibility that shooting would actually begin maybe over some mistaken sort of situation. But it didn't. I don't know how much influence the Tuscaloosa News had on the situation, but there weren't any major injuries to anyone during all this period.

Question: What was the black-white situation in Tuscaloosa before the Lucy incident?

Boone: It was a very interesting one. The relationship between people like myself and the young lady who came in to clean up our house was excellent. White Southerners who knew Negroes individually liked them to the extent that they would fight you over them. I mean if you come to a man's farm and started abusing a black man who worked for him, he would probably get his shotgun and run you off. The black man wouldn't have to. But as a group the Southern white men didn't trust the Negro. They considered him dirty, considered him slovenly, considered him inferior mentally.... The Southern white person loved his Negro friends and neighbors, meaning most of the people who worked with him, but didn't like the Negroes as a group.

Question: Was Lucy then a symbol of the change between the races, a symbol of the fact that now black people wanted to be equal to white people and a symbol that was very hard for the whites to understand...?

Boone: That's it exactly. She was a symbol and the white attitude was that we've absolutely got to keep this girl out of the University because if she stays another one is coming. I went back to Georgia, my neighbor state, and my brother-in-law said, "What is the matter with you people over there, you let this nigger girl in the University," and I said, "Bill, she was standing on the steps and we had to let her in or kill her." He looked sort of shook and he said, "Well, we ain't never going to have nothing like that happen over in Georgia." Now that was a typical Southern attitude.

Question: Wasn't the Lucy case tied up in the courts for quite a while? She only went (to the University) for three days.

Boone: She was expelled by the Board of Trustees.

Question: How long was it before the next attempt at desegregation?

Boone: In '63. That was Wallace's stand on the school. You remember Wallace's standing at the schoolhouse door. The student was Vivian Malone and the University integrated her very successfully.

Question: Did your paper take the same stand that it took with Autherine Lucy?

Boone: Yes, very strongly. But, before Wallace stood in the schoolhouse door I went with several people in Tuscaloosa to other places in the state to try to build up a demand that we be given some protection here in Tuscaloosa to handle properly what was going to come up. Wallace was not making any move whatever to provide any kind of police protection for the University or for Tuscaloosa, and we sat here as patsies for all of the Ku Klux Klan elements in the whole Southeast just waiting to be invaded. I even went to Oxford, Mississippi, with a group of people to talk with the Mississippi people to see what moves they had made over

54

there..... All of this was done behind the scenes. You have no idea how much behind the scenes work I did...trying to keep the lid on; trying to keep trouble from erupting.

Question: Do you think this is the role of a newspaper editor?

Boone: ...Yes, as a citizen of the community who was interested in the community and who loved all of his people.

Question: So you feel there is a point at which objectivity of the journalist must stop and personal involvement becomes very important?

Boone: Involvement is definitely important.

Question: But the pieces that were published in the newspaper at the time were a very straightforward kind of journalism.

Boone: I appreciate that comment. That's exactly what we were working to do. The instructions to our staff were very simple and very specific. "If it happens, cover it; if it's sensational, handle it as big stuff. Don't sensationalize the news; don't play it down. Write what occurs. If it's worth front page, put it on the front page. If it's worth a streamer, put it on a streamer." We did not in any single instance tell them to underplay or overplay anything. We tried to work as professionals.

Question: Did you lose business from advertisers because you took a moderate stand?

Boone: I am sure that I did but it didn't amount to much.

Question: Was there an organized campaign to boycott your paper?

Boone: Yes, but it was not made by advertisers. It was made by...subscribers.

Question: How many subscriptions did you lose?

Boone: I don't remember. During the Autherine Lucy situation there was so much happening that our circulation went up.

Question: How much was your circulation at that time?

Boone: It was around 16,000 or 17,000. We had one man in our circulation department--he left under unpleasant circumstances--and he went to work on a Birmingham newspaper. He went out to one of the local Goodrich plants during the height of this situation and as people came out he buttonholed them and he said, "Have you cancelled your subscription to the Tuscaloosa News yet? I'd like to start the Birmingham paper for you." The people at the Birmingham paper found out about it and they told him that if he continued to do this they would fire him. The Birmingham paper was our principal competition, of course, and those people up there conducted themselves on such a basis that I went up and thanked them after it was over. They refused to take any advantage whatever of their smaller competitor down here.

Question   How did it happen that you personally developed such a respect for law and order that you were willing to speak up for it?

Boone: I've always been able and willing to do that. I also spent four years as an FBI agent. I had a very profound respect for J. Edgar Hoover. I knew him personally. The last time I visited him in the Justice Building, about 15 years ago, I was invited into his office and I have been deeply grieved by some of the information that has come out about him. I don't say that I disbelieve it. He was an egotistical man who stayed too long in a position...and he made the mistake of making himself an institution which could do no wrong instead of a servant of the people.

Boone: But, you see there are principally two or three kinds of newspaper publishers. There is a...career newspaper publisher who comes up through the news and editorial department, and that was my situation. There is a publisher who is a professional newspaperman who comes up through the business office and who may or may not have a keen awareness of the responsibility of a newspaper from an editorial standpoint; and there is a man with money who made the money elsewhere or who inherited it who becomes a newspaper publisher and who may be a good editor-publisher or he may not. I wrote these editorials because I like to write, because I was the man with the final responsibility, and because the man who had the title of editor was from New Jersey and I felt that it would be better for a man who was born in the South to speak up on these things than for a man who was transplanted from New Jersey.

Boone: To give you an example of the sort of thing that went on, a friend saw me after the Rotary meeting one day and in a group said, "Boone, why do you refer to this nigger woman as Miss Lucy?" I said, "Mr. Pitt, we don't know any better way to designate an unmarried woman." And he said, "Well, some of us old Southerners don't like it." And I said "Well, let me tell you something, my great-grandfather was killed in the Battle of Bull Run, my grandfather on the other side was wounded in the war and if you can improve on that Southern background, just lay it on," and it shut him up. And somebody else said, "Yes, HIS family paid somebody to fight for them in Civil War." But there's an example of the sort of thinking. I believe the <u>Tuscaloosa News</u> was the first daily newspaper in the state to start using pictures of brides that were black and white. The first black bride that we ran was my daughter's classmate. We had worried for some weeks about it. The society editor had said, "Mr. Boone we will never have another white bride in our section if you run it," but we decided that we must do it. The paper came out and I can still remember my daughter's delight: "Mama, that's Ruby." We had very little reaction, but that was ten years after Autherine Lucy.

Question: You felt that you had a conscientious responsibility to lead the way for changes in the South?

Boone: I had a conscientious responsibility to take a position which would be right.

56

Question: So you felt that the typical Southern attitude toward blacks was wrong and it was time for change?

Boone: I thought it had to be. It has changed. To some extent my heritage goes along with that. My grandfather died in the '90s. When I would go to see him in Georgia, he would want to know what was happening in Alabama. He had been a leader in Georgia. He was a farmer; he had served in the legislature; he had been on the school board; and so forth. He told me in his later years that the time had to come when black people would have to be treated as human beings and so I guess he was to some extent influencing me. I was close to my grandfather, but he was much better educated than most of his peers.... One of the things that hurt him the most was that his brothers worked against him the last time he ran for the legislature because they were typical rednecks and he wasn't.

Boone: Our son was at the University when the Autherine Lucy incident occurred and the only comment I recall he made about it was that he hoped he never saw anything like it the rest of his life. It shocked him profoundly.

Question: Copenhagen offered Lucy a scholarship and she was offered opportunities to study at other universities in Europe. Were you embarrassed, as one who had a deep-seated Southern background, at the kinds of comments made about Tuscaloosa and the University at the time she left the school?

Boone: No, but our local people were. One of our town's finest citizens and one of my best friends came to me and said, "Isn't there any way you can stop printing these letters that come to the <u>Tuscaloosa News</u> that are saying how terrible the University and Tuscaloosa people are?" He said, "You published enough of them to give their viewpoint, so stop printing them because they aren't doing any good here." I said, "Well, how can I tell one man who expresses his opinion that his opinion is any less important than one that I have already printed. I can't. I have not declined to print a single letter."

Question: You felt that in publishing the letters you were helping your community move forward by showing them what outsiders thought of the community action?

Boone: I felt that in publishing the letters we were carrying out our policy of publishing letters, period. I didn't run an editorial page to try to achieve anything other than run a good newspaper....

Question: If you had any advice to offer the budding journalist today, or even a new editor, what would it be?

Boone: Don't try to needle people, or the community for that matter, just for the sake of needling. Don't try to create issues and confrontations simply for that, but stand on principle and speak up fairly, reasonably, and intelligently, and if people disagree with you, publish their views. There have been newspapers in this country that would not publish opposing views...but I have seen a vast improvement in the professional level of newspapers in this country since I entered the newspaper business back in 1929, a vast improvement.

WRITING SAMPLES:

BOONE

WHAT A PRICE FOR PEACE

(Editorial)

When mobs start imposing their frenzied will on universities, we have a bad situation.

But that is what has happened at the University of Alabama. And it is a development over which the University of Alabama, the people of this state and the community of Tuscaloosa should be deeply ashamed--and more than a little afraid.

Our government's authority springs from the will of the people. But their wishes, if we are to be guided by democratic processes, must be expressed by ballot at the polls, by action in the legislative halls, and finally by interpretation from the bench. No intelligent expression ever has come from a crazed mob, and it never will.

And make no mistake. There was a mob, in the worst sense, at the University of Alabama yesterday.

Every person who witnessed the events there with comparative detachment speaks of the tragic nearness with which our great University came to being associated with a murder--yes, we said murder.

"If they could have gotten their hands on her, they would have killed her."

That was the considered judgement, often expressed, of many who watched the action without participating in it.

The target was Authurine Lucy. Her "crimes?" She was born black, and she was moving against Southern custom and tradition--but with the law, right on up to the United States Supreme court, on her side.

What does it mean today at the University of Alabama, and here in Tuscaloosa, to have the law on your side?

The answer has to be: Nothing--that is, if a mob disagrees with you and the courts.

As matters now stand, the University administration and trustees have knuckled under to the pressures and desires of a mob. What is to keep the same mob, if uncontrolled again, from taking over in any other field where it decides to impose its wishes? Apparently, nothing.

What is the answer to a mob? We think that is clear. It lies in firm, decisive action. It lies in the use of whatever force is necessary to restrain and subdue anyone who is violating the law.

58

Not a single University student has been arrested on the campus and that is no indictment against the men in uniform, but against higher levels which failed to give them clear-cut authority to go along with responsibility.

What has happened here is far more important than whether a Negro girl is admitted to the University. We have a breakdown of law and order, an abject surrender to what is expedient rather than a courageous stand for what is right.

Yes, there's peace on the University campus this morning. But what a price has been paid for it!

February 7, 1956

Buford Boone

THE WISDOM OF PATIENCE

(Editorial)

Patience, described fittingly as a virtue, also is the mark of an intelligent man.

Many are the repercussions from the segregation problem that has racked the University of Alabama. But the institution will come through this crisis. It was burned down, once, but rose from the ashes of its wanton destruction stronger, more vigorous than ever.

Men make institutions. We are inclined to over-emphasize the problems that weigh down upon us. For to do less would detract from the importance we like to attach to ourselves.

But history will look back on the current period and judge with certainty that the human beings whose fate it was to live in these times had a problem that was made big by their own frailties--but nevertheless was big, and difficult, and had no ideal or quick solution.

What will those who chronicle the history of these times have to say about the faculty and the staff at the University? The answer to that question is being decided now.

At such times, men of good will who work honestly and earnestly through moderate approaches are misunderstood by the idealists (a better word than extremists). It is a time when Monday-morning quarterbacking is made more natural than ever, for in this instance we are playing the game of democracy and every one of us is a player-coach. But this is a game we can't afford to lose.

A 20-year-old student at the University, now in demand as a speaker for Citizens Council meetings over the state, apparently is furnishing the leadership for a "clean-out-from-top-to-bottom" movement. He means that he believes that all connected with the University who would make required adjustments or compromises forced by the inexorable pressure of legal decisions against our Southern customs and traditions should be fired.

On the other hand, some of the faculty members feel that we should move faster and do more in democratic realism. They are frowning on the University's record in the segregation crisis. Some, we know, are in serious contemplation of the action they should take to stand by their ideals.

We recognize the right to hold either view. Those are, to restate them: (1) That President Carmichael and any others at the University who have taken the position that our institution must follow the law of the land and must recognize the majesty of the courts ought to be fired; and (2) that the best course for an idealist who is a purist in his concept of democracy is to resign his connection with the University in protest.

60

The attitude of those who take the first position is so patently unfair, so unreasonable, and so extreme that we shall not comment upon it further, except on one point. We do suggest that 20-year-old wisdom isn't mature enough on a problem of this size and complication. We believe the second conclusion is premature and hasty. By taking such a course a faculty member would not be furthering the cause in which he believes.

The segregation issue, which will be in the forefront here in the South for many years, is one that will require the constant understanding, the perpetual patience, and the broad views of many to avoid unhappy events.

This is a time, we suggest, when the University needs its friends more than ever. We must be honest, we must be concerned, we must be critical if we can do so constructively. But there's room for every one of us who loves the University.

Perhaps that element will be a leavening influence that will work for good throughout the present and the future--for devotion to an institution is a fine thing. Certainly, a protest resignation will do little other than bring some measure of relief to the troubled individual taking the action.

We don't remember, in our history, men who walk out in protest. We remember the Benjamin Franklins who labor through days of patient toil, who accept disappointments, who make compromises--but who never stop working in seeking wise, fair and enduring solutions to problems that, to lesser men, seem insurmountable.

Freedom of mind is a precious thing. Ease of conscience is more important than creature comforts. But time is the best palliative in this problem. We have more of it to invest, perhaps, than we sometimes realize. Quick decisions may be incorrect decisions.

So we suggest to the members of the University faculty who may be understandably restive because of the recent developments that we know of nothing surpassing the wisdom of patience at a time like this. Such an attitude does make certain that whatever decisions are made in individual cases will be thought out well, instead of being hasty.

March 7, 1956

Buford Boone

TIME TO TAKE A STAND

(Editorial)

The Tuscaloosa Council on Human Relations has performed a needed public service in acting as a community conscience and in calling upon top elements of leadership here to stand for maintenance of law and order.

The council is the first and only group to face up publicly to the possibility that difficulties may develop again at the University of Alabama in the fall and to urge the handling of whatever problems may arise without resort to violence and outside-the-law activity.

The council is made up of about 50 members, both white and Negro. As an organization, it does not have the power and influence that some other local groups possess. But it has called attention to a vacuum of responsible leadership in dealing with community reaction to possible racial discord in the fall. In doing so, it has discharged a responsibility and at the same time it has issued a challenge to those in positions of constitutional authority, religious influence and civic weight.

If Negro students should seek admission to the University of Alabama in September, as they have a right to do under court order, this community again would find itself spotlighted. University administrators again would find themselves between the pressures of public opinion against any breakdown in segregation and court orders based upon Supreme Court interpretation of the United States Constitution.

We may not have Negro applicants at the University in the fall. But if we do not at that time, we are certain to have some apply later. If they are qualified, they must be admitted or the court's order must be disobeyed, as matters now stand.

Whatever may be a person's viewpoint on the overall issue, we have to face up to the question of how we are going to react to a situation where fellow citizens are taking advantage of constitutional rights affirmed by federal tribunals.

As matters now stand, our community's reaction is being left to a strong Ku Klux Klan and a stronger Citizens Council. Their leaders have affirmed repeatedly, and laudably, their determination to use lawful measures only in supporting their view that no change whatever is to be tolerated in the segregation picture. Are the members of these groups, an important segment of our community, being realistic in their attitude since the courts have ruled? And will the leaders be able to hold their memberships in line on the sound stand against violence?

If the local elected authorities, the civic leaders, the business organizations and our ministers are satisfied to go along with the Klansmen and Council members, then we are all set for the fall. If,

63

however, there is a feeling that some more realistic preparation must be
made to build a foundation of support under law enforcement; if our
officers are to be given greater assurance that the people want law and
order and will support action to maintain it--then steps such as the
Council on Human Relations suggests are needed.

Thus far, responsible community leaders have taken no public action
in support of law and order and against the sort of lawlessness that
existed on the campus for a time last February.

Up to now, the trustees of the University have made no public
statement, in anticipation of fall problems. So far as the public knows,
the trustees have left the University administration between the strong
pressure against change and the necessity of compliance with court
orders.

We share the Council on Human Relations' confidence in the stability
and ability of our community's leadership. But isn't it about time we
were taking some steps?

July 19, 1956

Buford Boone

...a bullet through your stupid head!

IRA B. HARKEY, JR.
Pascagoula (Miss.) Chronicle
Pulitzer Prize—Editorial Writing
1963

5

In Mississippi during the 1960's, those who dared to espouse anything other than complete segregation of blacks and whites were likely to become social outcasts.

One pariah was Ira B., Harkey Jr., editor and publisher of the Chronicle in Pascagoula, Mississippi, a Gulf Coast shipbuilding and fishing town. Harkey supported James Meredith in his efforts to become the first black to attend the University of Mississippi. This made Harkey the chief target of the 600-member Jackson County Citizens Emergency Unit, a white supremacist group organized to uphold segregation.

As Mississippi appeared unable to cope with a violent reaction to desegregation, Harkey spoke almost alone in his community on the side of upholding the law and integrating the University. Harkey's liberal stand was not a new one. He was one of the first Mississippi journalists to use Mr. and Mrs. before the names of blacks and to print their photographs. He objected to the contemptuous term "nigger" and was outraged by the violation of human dignity perpetuated when newspapers ran headlines such as "Two Men and a Negro Killed in Auto Accident."

Unsupported by most of his colleagues in the Mississippi press, Harkey withstood economic seige and physical threats. In two months, the Chronicle lost five large advertisers and its circulation dropped from 7,000 to 6,200. The threats were equally intimitating: A bullet through the newspaper door; a shotgun blast through the window of his home; hate-filled letters; and the classic Klan warning, a cross burning on his lawn.

65

Harkey continued to fight intolerance with his only weapon, the editorial. And he and the <u>Chronicle</u> prevailed: The Citizens Emergency Unit was disbanded, the newspaper survived and desegregation came. But through it all, Harkey received support chiefly from only one person among the 54,000 residents of Jackson County - Claude Ramsey, state president of the AFL-CIO. The labor leader pointed out that racial unrest in Pascagoula might cost the nearby Ingall's shipyard government contracts, with resultant economic loss to the community.

As Harkey said, he won and lost at the same time. Despite the return of circulation and advertisers to the <u>Chronicle</u>, the editor was a pariah. In December 1963, six months after receiving the Pulitzer prize in editorial writing, he sold the <u>Chronicle</u> and left Mississippi. He detailed his experiences in an autobiography, <u>The Smell of Burning Crosses</u>, published in 1967.

Born in New Orleans in 1918, Harkey said in one editorial that a non-Southerner cannot "understand the full terror of a cross burning, this classic threat from the Klan. It is like the voice of doom, the sentence of death, the placing of the victim beyond the pale." Following the cross burning of his lawn, he hailed the new fall season in an editorial beginning, "Ah, autumn! Falling leaves...the hint of the north breeze stirring in the night...the smell of burning crosses in the air...."

After graduation from Tulane University in New Orleans, Harkey was a reporter and feature writer for the New Orleans <u>Times-Picayune</u>, with his career interrupted by service as a lieutenant in the U.S. Navy during World War II. In 1949, he fulfilled his dream of owning a newspaper by acquiring the Pascagoula <u>Chronicle</u>, which he converted from a weekly to a daily, and a printing company.

Following sale of the newspaper Harkey taught at Ohio State University where he received master's and doctor's degrees in political science. He also has taught at the University of Alaska, the University of Montana and the University of Oregon. His book, <u>Pioneer Bush Pilot</u>, the story of an Alaskan pilot, appeared in 1974.

In addition to the Pulitzer prize, he received awards for his editorials from the Sidney Hillman Foundation, the National Conference of Christians and Jews and the Society of Professional Journalists. Harkey is a vice-president and director of the Oklahoma Coca-Cola Bottling Co. and a director of Sequin Aviation. He has been married three times and is the father of seven children.

Harkey himself described the events surrounding Meredith's attempt to enter the University in an introduction to a pamphlet containing his Pulitzer prize editorials. He wrote:

On the night of September 13, 1962, Gov. Ross Barnett of Mississippi broadcast a statewide radio and television message. He announced his defiance of U.S. efforts to obtain admission of Mississippian James Meredith, a Negro, to the University of Mississippi. He vowed that Ole Miss would never be integrated, thrust himself between the nation and the state in a buffer zone he termed "interposition," called upon all Mississippians to resist and demanded the resignation of public officials not eager to follow him in defiance.

The next day, the Pascagoula Chronicle published the state's first editorial expression of disapproval of the stand Barnett had adopted. On September 19, when a second editorial opposing Barnett appeared, The Chronicle drew sneering notice from a state capital daily as "the only newspaper to oppose the chartered course of Mississippi."

The tragedy predicted in the Chronicles's first two editorials occurred the night of September 30 when mobs battled U.S. marshals, soldiers and Mississippi National Guardsmen on the Ole Miss campus after Meredith had been admitted to the university.

During the next few weeks, while state leaders, cheered to the echo by an almost unanimous (and almost hysterical) press, called down blame on every U.S. official from Chief Marshal McShane to the President. The Chronicle said the blame rested with Mississippi's politicians and the jungle of hate they had cultivated.

Early in October, a group of Pascagoula-area men who had armed themselves and followed their sheriff to Ole Miss the day of the riots, formed a permanent organization, the Jackson County Citizens Emergency Unit. It was organized under sponsorship of the sheriff, who presided at early meetings in the Courthouse, of which he is custodian. The announced purpose of its "action committee" was to "take care of nigger-lovers so that we're not embarrassed like the people of Oxford were."

Its first target, announced at a meeting attended by a Chronicle reporter, was to be the Chronicle, branded by the sheriff and Unit leaders as the leading "nigger-lover," which "ridicules" the governor, calls Negroes "Mr." and "Mrs." and does not identify people by race in its news columns. After a nighttime pistol shot broke out a two-foot section of the Chronicle's plate glass door, the Chronicle ran a front-page editorial and continued its counterattack with others.

Although several leading citizens privately deplored the Emergency Unit's purposes, none would make a public statement. The sheriff's sponsorship of the Unit made it almost impossible for the Chronicle to obtain help from other local police organizations. But despite this isolation, a flood of hate mail and phone calls, personal ostracism of the Chronicle editor and staff, a boycott placed against the paper's advertisers, threats to carrierboys, and a shotgun blast that blew out the windows in the editor's office, the Chronicle continued to speak.

As many as 400 persons attended weekly meetings of the Emergency Unit. (The sheriff claimed 600.) KKK members from nearby Alabama, Citizens Council people from as far as 100 miles away, attended. "Maneuvers" were scheduled for Saturday mornings under direction of a "training officer."

The only person to speak publicly in favor of the Chronicle was Claude Ramsay, a Jackson County resident and president of the Mississippi

Labor Council AFL-CIO. The U.S. Justice Department announced in Washington that it had ordered the FBI to conduct an investigation to determine if the civil rights of the _Chronicle's_ editor were being violated.

As the year drew to a close, several officers of the Emergency Unit resigned. An attorney who said he had acted only to draw up a charter on request of the sheriff, announced he had no connection with the Unit. Meetings continued to be held every Monday night but attendance shrank from more than 400 to less than 30 hard-core haters.

Christmas was near when the editorial headed "How many kinds of Christianity?" appeared. It aroused much comment. One response was a letter to the editor from a woman employed by a local library. She wrote that if a clipping she enclosed was not published, "instead of a bullet through your door I hope you get a bullet through your stupid head." This letter, as were all others received during the _Chronicle's_ four-month ordeal, was published in the paper. As no protest was voiced that a woman in such a job could hold and express such a sentiment, it may be assumed that she spoke the mind of the city.

HARKEY INTERVIEW

Question: What first kindled your interest in the topic for which you received the Pulitzer prize?

Harkey: I won the Pulitzer Prize for editorial writing following the riots at the University of Mississippi after the admission of James Meredith, in October, 1962. Now what first kindled my interest in the topic (was that) I was a wide-eyed kid who believed what he heard in Sunday School about brotherhood, and...second, just reading, I love to read history, I love to read biographies. I read biographies about great Americans...and I think I got some idea of the concept of what democracy and Americanism is. And this made no mention of appearance, accidental appearance.... Third, the war (World War II). It was ironic for me to see that we buried 52 people at one time--tossed them over the side (of a Navy ship on which he served)--and some were black people. It suddenly struck me...where are they going? Are they going to go to a restricted heaven someplace that said "all the colored people - step to the rear," or "white only." Then I had some friends from Oklahoma, and a Frenchman who taught at Xavier University, and while I was in college,...I think talking with them for the three or four years that I knew them,...changed my mind and Southern attitude. So, during the war, I was working as a newspaperman...and what I wanted to do was to get into a little newspaper in the deep South and see if I could promote my ideas, and perhaps do some good. Now this is an idealistic, and it turned out, witless ambition or endeavor.

Question: You said you had a Southerner's attitude before that. Will you expound on that?

Harkey: It's a very difficult thing to do - to explain - "how do you get that way?" I don't know.... I used to listen to my great-grandmother,...tell stories of the Civil War and there never were any "damn Yankees" in it; never was any hatred and rancor - and they (great-grandparents) went through hell; they were burned out and so on, but there was no hatred and there was never anything about the blacks in it. I never heard them say "nigger." In our family we never used "nigger!" My mother didn't allow it. My father's from the middle of Mississippi and when I was a very little boy I remember occasionally he would say that and my mother would correct him.... If we would hear people on the street and come home and say it, mother said, "We don't talk like this, Christian ladies and gentlemen don't say that word." Later on, all my friends were typical white Southerners, and...there was no other word, no other way to refer to a black man, but "nigger." There simply was no other way, and of course, they didn't mean it as a slurring word.

Question: What is the typical Southern attitude?

Harkey: The typical white Southerner of the lower economic class is brought up with a certain hatred, he's competitive with blacks, he has almost nothing else he can look down upon, and this is his scapegoat - black men. The white is better, no matter what he is, say he's a thieving, drunken bum, he's better than any "Goddamn nigger" that ever lived. The people of the upper middle income groups are not taught this hatred, but they are taught that the blacks are subhuman.... And they pride themselves in taking care of their neighbors,...looking so kind they can't understand all the screaming about...lynching somebody or doing harm. But because of what they say, they give support to those who do these things, and the Klansman is the typical guy who didn't go beyond the third grade and he sometimes can't spell cat. His economic level is filling station operator and sometimes he may work for himself.

Question: What sort of audience did you have?

Harkey: The same. It was a good audience, I thought, because the Gulf Coast is a bit more liberal and intimate. I got shot at on the Coast; I would absolutely have been blown to bits if I had been thirty miles inland. Where I went (Pascagoula) was a little fishing and shipbuilding community. There never had been big plantations there; they never had had a majority of black people. So there were slight differences in attitudes. And there was a rather sizable Roman Catholic community and I thought this would be helpful.... Well, I wanted to tell the right side, that the black man was a human being and he was deserving from his government of the same darn things that everyone else gets, without regard to whether they're six feet tall or have red hair, blue eyes, big feet, little feet or wherever. And I thought it would be possible to do this. I realize it was ridiculous...because it simply was not possible.

Harkey: The newspaper I bought used to say, "Billy Jones, colored," so on and so forth, "Maggie Jones, colored" and such things as "two people and a colored maid were killed in an automobile accident." Anyway, I dropped the tag. Another thing, there never was a story in this paper about a black man that wasn't a police story. There never was anything about a black person doing anything but getting into trouble. I started doing little features about them. Dropped the tag. I started Negro with a capital N. Now, this was revolutionary. "This was communistic."

Question: Was the term black used?

Harkey: Oh, black! This was the most ironic thing. The blacks now want to be black! But, by God, in those days black was worse than nigger, because the only way it went was "black bastard!" It's ironic because that was worse, really, than nigger. Anyway, eventually I dropped the tag completely, and didn't use any except when it was pertinent, and I justified it on the journalistic principle that you don't put in facts that are irrelevant to a story. In a fugitive story, the fact that he's black is relevant, just as what he's wearing is relevant, his height and weight, and so on, and the kind of car he's in, so I would do it that way but not in any other way. Then I started using "Mrs." for married Negro women and this was considered awful.

Question: Was no formal address used?

Harkey: No, just first names. You see, Maggie Washington was "Maggie." Maggie Washington was referred to later on as Maggie, or the maid, or the colored woman. I got into such hell with this that I decided, okay, I'm going to drop all honorifics for everybody, so we're now going to be blacks and whites alike, we're not going to be Miss, Mrs. and Mr. and so we will be consistent. I dropped doctor for instance, when it wasn't relevant to the story.

Question: I imagine a few people were a bit upset?

Harkey: Well, to the doctors around town it was terrible not to be called Doctor!...in Mississippi the wives of MDs called themselves "Mrs. Doctor." You see the man's name changes when he becomes a doctor. He's no longer Wintrop Smith - he's Doctor and that's part of it.

Harkey: I thought that over the years I could do some good, as I say, and when this showdown came - and I knew it was inevitable--everybody knew--the whole thing is civil rights! And then when...Martin Luther King joined and organized the Southern Conference, it became absolutely apparent that it had to be solved or it would blow up the country. And I thought that my people, in my little leadership, would have the advantage. It was an economic stupidity to have duplicate school systems for blacks and whites and each to be not worth a nickel.

Harkey: You see, I was there for 14 years, 1949 on and so I was...trying to promote the idea that the black man is human, he's an American citizen and he is worth exactly what the white man is, (and it is) his government too and that it was economic stupidity to deny that it was. And if this (segregation) was not anti-Christian it was certainly unChristian.

Harkey: You see, these guys (the whites) go to church all the time.... And they'll kill you. But they're in the church and the church is their club. And you talk about it in the club...you talk about charity and that means charity for us and people like us (the whites). Brotherhood - that means people like us. I used to enrage them. I said a Communist is a guy who talks Christianity out on the streets, away from the church, and this is true.

Question: You did this, not only in the paper, but personally?

Harkey: Yes. My pressman was a black man and he got the same wages as anybody else did, but this was unheard of. See, you gave the black man just as little as you possibly could. I couldn't have protected a black reporter. He would have been killed the first time he walked into somebody's front door. But people--individuals would tell me, "We're sure glad you're here. This is a fine thing you're doing, just want to tell you...." (But) they would never ask the Kessler Air Force Base in Biloxi to come march in parades because they had black guys. They couldn't have black marching with white. They couldn't have the glee club come sing because there were blacks in the glee club. But lo and behold over the years they started doing those things.... Anyway, we're getting way off the track. What was the background? Well,...the actual background was the admission of James Meredith to the University of Mississippi.... The governor was actually so stupid that he thought he could prevent this.

Question: Did you work alone?

Harkey: Alone? Hell, yes. Half the people working for me wouldn't speak to me. There was a lot of yelling in the office and side taking.... It's a wonder we were able to keep going.

Harkey: I was being told by people that they agreed with me and they thought it was wonderful that I would actually do this fine work. All sorts of people--people I wouldn't even think could read, much less could think that way.... But when the showdown came, everyone disappeared. Except one guy, a labor leader - Claude Ramsey (the President of the Mississippi AFL-CIO). A really great guy, a great man.

Question: You were essentially forced to leave - weren't you?

Harkey: It's hard to say. I had been approached for years to sell the paper.... The real truth of it is...I wanted to get out of Mississippi to get a divorce.... I had won the fight, really. It was all over. The circulation was coming back--I had lost only about 12%--the outfit that had 600 to 700 in it - the mob - led by the sheriff, had dwindled down to nothing but a couple of nuts; the advertising started coming back. I had lost a whole year's profit - had gone in the hole. I had a bodyguard. I had moved into a hotel and all sorts of things.

Question: How long did you have to live that way?

Harkey: About four months. But I had lost only about 12% of the circulation. They (the local citizens) still wanted to see what the little bastard was saying. But the advertising was just down to nothing. They took the papers away from the carriers, knocked the carriers down and threatened the advertisers.

Question: One of the editorials you wrote mentioned pressure on your advertisers by this group, the Johnson County Citizens Emergency Unit.

Harkey: I had to put a little more optimism in that sort of editorial than I really felt. I couldn't say we had lost a year's profits, we can't go very much longer. I couldn't possibly say that. But the circulation only dropped a little. As I said, they wanted to see what the heck was going on. And it was lovely to hear them say, "Did you hear what so and so said?" And out in my own office, the ad manager would get red in the face when he'd read my editorials.

Question: How many people worked for the paper at that time?

Harkey: About 40, including the people who handled the paper and distributed it. We had a good shop...a union shop. And I wanted it that way, because you got good people.

Question: Were you the only paper in that area or did you have competition?

Harkey: I had competition for about two years. The man I bought the paper from started another paper. Then he sold it back to some people after they saw the way I was turning out - "Communist" and so on. And, I've got the damnedest Mississippi credentials you ever heard of. My grandmother was a Millsap--and...being a Millsap from Mississippi, you can't beat that. They said, "He's a Yankee" and they said, "No, he's not a Yankee, he's from here." They were trying to make some excuse for what was wrong with me. Then they said, "Well, he went away to school - he went up North to school." Then they said, "Well, his parents are Yankees." No, his grandmother was a Millsap, his father was born in Scott County, his mother was born in Knoxville, Tennessee." "Well, he married a Yankee."

Question: Did you?

Harkey: No! It was really funny. It used to infuriate me. I'd say, "I was born further south than any of you people, I was born in New Orleans."

Question: Did mostly Jackson County people read your paper?

Harkey: Yes. The two papers (from the State Capital at Jackson) had the biggest outside circulation. Boy, if you ever want to see hate - look back on some of those papers!

Question: But yours must have had some influence?

Harkey: Well, I don't know. I don't know that I changed anybody's opinions. A lot of people told me I did, but they didn't act on them and certainly after the Meredith riots, nobody told me after that, until Claude Ramsey. Ramsey started the only way he could by saying, "Look we've got to stop this. We're all going to lose our jobs, because the federal government is going to come in here and take these contracts away (from the local shipyard)." They were all working at the shipyard on federal contracts, and so he used the dollar approach, which I used, too.

Question: Did you constantly employ certain writing techniques to make and emphasize your point?

Harkey: I kept beating on their Christianity, and then economics. There are two points to this. In general, writing an editorial should be short. There's nothing drearier than twelve inches of three columns of grey items. There should be short paragraphs. The opening should say what the writer is going to talk aobut. "The mayor is a crook," then the next thing it should say is why the mayor is a crook, then at the end, repeat what you were going to talk about, "Therefore the mayor is a crook" and stop. In general, that's the way an editorial should be written. I had some experiences trying to be satirical and being taken literally. If you try satire and you don't somehow signal it to your reader it is misunderstood. So, with satire, you had to go easy unless you could slapstick it so that anyone could realize that it was satire.

Question: What does "good writing" mean?

Harkey: Good writing is writing that people read, as far as an editorial goes. I wrote a daily column and it was humorous, hate is humorous, and people thought I was funny, and so they used to read what I had to write. And the editorial was three columns wide set at 10 point, and if that can be appetizing, it's appetizing. You're going to read that. Great big head! Lot of white space like an attractive ad. Seven paragraphs, only one long paragraph, occasionally two bold-face paragraphs is good display and it's attractive to the eye. If that had been three times that long, very few people would read it.

Question: Getting back to what we were talking about. You're not really sure whether you left there because of all the trouble or for other reasons?

Harkey: The thing was over. This outfit (the mob) had disappeared. Oh, all the hate was there still and I was a pariah. Nobody would be seen talking to me. Maybe this is rationalizing again. If I'd been a real fanatic I'd have stayed. I'd made my try and all the people I thought were with me had evaporated at the time that I needed them.... If there'd been another sheriff.... You see, the sheriff there sent out the call for all patriots...all the red blooded Americans, "Southern Americans," (You don't need to say white, because that's assumed), to meet at the court house. And they went up, and they bragged about how they'd raised more hell (at the University), and fired off more ammunition than anybody else. Seven hundred of them. Another sheriff, another man, might not have done that, and there would have been no such idiot to rally them in the community. Suppose that hadn't happened? I don't know if that would have affected the Pulitzer Prize! It's supposed to be for writing.... But, when you send your exhibit to the committee you have to explain, just like I'm explaining now, so they knew what had happened. And of course it was in the papers. And radio and TV stations were calling from all over the country asking for interviews, and Barbara Walters wanted to get me to come up to do the <u>Today Show</u>, and I said "That would get me killed for sure, if I showed up." You see, they'll tape it, but with all this recognition, and going out to the North and gloating about it, and really rubbing it in, that would have been awful.

Question: Were you disillusioned by the whole thing; didn't you just feel like giving up and going away?

Harkey: Well, I didn't want to continue to live like that. I had no friends. The only friend I made had died a couple of years before.... A person I could talk to about my hopes and aspirations...and he reciprocated. Now, the ones I had talked with who had indicated that they thought as I did, had been persuaded, and were glad I was there and proud of the fine newspaper, all disappeared, as I said. There was one guy who came in and said he was all with me, but, "For God's sake don't tell Polly,"--his wife--"Don't ever tell her I came in."

Question: So, it was just, kind of, over - or did you feel driven out?

Harkey: Well, I can't let myself feel driven out. I do feel guilty about not being there later on, but I definitely feel that I ran out - to some extent - that I ran out on the situation, that I should have stayed a little bit longer. I never would have left while this group--the mob--was in attendance there, I never could have left then. I had won, they had disappeared, physically disappeared.... I still could have stayed, but the main thing was to get my private life settled. This had been a hell of an experience--four months of very harrowing experiences.

WRITING SAMPLES:

HARKEY

GOVERNOR REACHES POINT OF NO RETURN

(Editorial)

Mississippians are mature enough to recognize the inevitable, to accept it and adapt to it with good enough grace. The political faction that rules them, however, is not.

We had always thought deep down inside that when the moment arrived even Ross Barnett and his blazing advisors would make the best of it.

Instead, the emotional nature of Barnett's address last night left little doubt that he intends to make the worst of it. He will drive Mississippi to chaos.

True, the exact "moment" has not yet arrived. Barnett last night invoked the "doctrine of interposition," attempting to place the sovereignty of the state between state officials and the U.S. government, thus removing the necessity of their complying with federal orders to admit James Meredith to Ole Miss.

If the governor had stopped there, perhaps there would still be hope that ruin could be avoided. But he went far beyond an invocation of interposition. He called upon officials to defy the United States and he vowed again that Ole Miss would not be integrated. This can mean only one thing, that when interposition is brushed aside in the courts--as the bogus contention surely will -- Barnett either will back down or will destroy our educational system. His words last night make it virtually impossible for him to back down.

It is too early yet to attempt an analysis of Barnett's address to determine what else was in it. This was in it, though: a dangerous use of the century's most inflammatory issue in an attempt to solidify Brand X power in Mississippi. This attempt was proclaimed when he dragged in his whipping boy "the Kennedy administration" and said "the Kennedy administration is lending the power of the federal government to the ruthless demands of...agitators."

But it is not "the Kennedy administration" that is making demands upon Mississippi. It is the United States of America, it is democracy itself, it is the whole of humanity. These surely will not back down either. Barnett has asked them to force us to comply. They will, and the process can ruin Mississippi.

September 14, 1962   Ira B. Harkey

78

CONFUSING TIMES, DANGEROUS TIMES

(Editorial)

A pall of contradiction covers our state as if every one of us had developed schizophrenia.

The newspapers and politicians who hailed Gov. Barnett's address call upon citizens not to resort to violence. "Do they really mean it?" is the question, for these same papers and people have long been advocates of a "fight to the finish" and now they may see just what it is they have raised up. How can we defy the law "to the finish" without resorting to violence?

Then there is the call upon the United States of America not to send marshals into our state to enforce tne law. How can we make such a demand without appearing devoid of all sense? Does the burglar announce to the police that he will not observe anti-burgling statutes because they violate his way of life and then expect the police to issue him an exemption?

Gov. Barnett knows full well how laws are enforced when the lawless are defiant. He himself has sent troops into counties to search out a bottle of whiskey here, to shatter a crap table there. Federal marshals enforce the law except in rebellions which are tended to by troops. How do we think that the United States will enforce the law now? By sending in the Peace Corps? Postmen? Soil conservationists? When orders are ignored, force is applied. Gov. Barnett knows that.

A Sunday editorial in a state capital paper is titled "Future Economic Growth Hinges on State Income Conditioners," as if there will be any growth but of hate, any conditioners but strife, any state income but grief in the turmoil of anarchy we are approaching.

At a lunch meeting Monday at beautiful Longfellow House in Pascagoula a group of local leaders heard a talk by a Mississippi State University official. He spoke on plans the university has for its educational program in Jackson County--as if there will be any education after Ole Miss has been padlocked or burned down or whatever it is Gov. Barnett has planned for it.

Meanwhile, the first Mississippian to decline Gov. Barnett's invitation to go to jail is Judge Sidney Mize of Gulfport. The day after the governor's speech, Mize issued an order directing Ole Miss to admit James Meredith without delay. Mize followed instructions of the federal circuit court of appeals rather than Gov. Barnett's call to suicide.

In a madhouse's din, Mississippi waits. God help Mississippi.

September 20, 1962   Ira B. Harkey

IF GOONS THREATEN YOU, HERE IS WHAT TO DO

(Editorial)

Four Chronicle advertisers report that they have been instructed not to do business with the newspaper. Others may be afraid to report.

This is what the Jackson County Citizens Emergency unit said it would do--"put the pressure on Chronicle advertisers."

If they continue to advertise, the businessmen reported, the goons said they "will not be responsible for anything that happens to your business."

One strongarm man threatened an advertiser by saying he represented "a union of 300 families" that would boycott the store.

For the reasurrance of Chronicle advertisers we offer this:

o   Threats of physical violence are illegal and evidence is being gathered that will take care of goons that make such treats.

o   There are not 300 families in Jackson County so low in morals that they would condone much less participate in such an attack against anyone. If there are 300 such, their economic status is so depressed that their buying-power is nothing.

o   If you are threatened or even talked to about dropping your advertising in the Chronicle, call the Chronicle immediately and give us the name of the goon, his description and a report of what he said.

o   Decent, law-abiding businessmen...have nothing to fear. Right is on your side, help is coming and we assure you that our community will not be allowed to succumb to dictation by evil elements that would destroy all that is good in our lives.

October 29, 1962

Ira B. Harkey

HOW MANY KINDS OF CHRISTIANITY?

(Editorial)

Well, certainly, the governor's cousin is correct when she complains that the racial attitudes of her native state's leaders make more difficult her job as a missionary in Nigeria.

"You send us out here to preach that Christ died for all men," wrote Antonina Canzoneri to a Mississippi Baptist newspaper, "then you make a travesty of our message by refusing to associate with some of them because of the color of their skin."

This is the basic cause of the Mississippi schizophrenia, the incredible disease that allows us to claim that we are at one and the same time Christians and white supremists, when there are no two attitudes more incompatible than these.

The racists would have you believe that the teachings of Christ, the lessons you learned in Sunday school, are like the Santa Claus myth, just something to kid around with. The Sermon on the Mount, the brotherhood of men in God, the great philosophy of kindness and compassion, all of this just words to listen to on Sunday and then forget at the door of the church.

Christianity is a white man's fraternity, they impute. There is only one God, but he is God only for certain people, people who look and think like we do. There is a heaven, but there would have to be a sign by the pearly gates that says "All Colored Angels Step to the Rear," where they will find a heaven-annex marked "For Our Colored Patrons Only."

Christianity is a philosophy of tolerance, a philosophy that makes bearable through hope the wretched lives of the unprivileged. It is a philosophy of love and understanding and turn the other cheek. It is a philosophy that makes no sense on a once a week basis, that is barren and futile if shucked at the door of the church and not carried out into the world and practiced there.

In Mississippi, a person who attempts to carry Christianity out the church door, who dares to practice the Christian virtue of tolerance outside the church, is cursed as liberal, a leftist, a communist, a niggerlover. Christ was the greatest champion of the underdog the world has ever known. If He were to visit us here, now, by whose side would He stand, beside the brick-throwing, foulmouthed, destroying, profaning, slavering members of the mob and their "nice-folk" eggers-on, or beside the trembling victim of their hate?

There cannot be one answer for Sunday between 11 a.m. and noon and another for the rest of the week. And there cannot be one brand of Christianity for Mississippi and another for Nigeria and the rest of the world.

Christmas, 1962   Ira B. Harkey   81

Hell, no, I'm not trying to start
a riot, I'm trying to stop one!

HAZEL BRANNON SMITH
Lexington (Miss.) Advertiser
Pulitzer Prize—Editorial Writing
1964

6

Holmes County, Mississippi, where the flat, black land of the Delta meets the hill country of the small farmer and sawmill owner, lies apart from the mainstream of American life. Isolated geographically and culturally, Holmes County has been dominated for generations by plantation feudalism and provincial fears rooted in past hostilities. In the midst of this repressive atmosphere, a newspaper publisher, Hazel Brannon Smith, waged a long-fought battle to preserve freedom of the press.

Smith moved to Holmes County in 1936, with a fresh journalism degree from the University of Alabama and a dream of owning her own newspaper. Using a borrowed $3,000 she took over a failing weekly, the Durant News, and soon took on the civic establishment. Vowing to let decent citizens know what was going on, she exposed corrupt officials allied with slot machine operators, liquor racketeers and gamblers. Working around-the-clock, she made a success of her first newspaper and in 1943 bought the Advertiser, Mississippi's second oldest newspaper, in Lexington, the county seat. Later she added two more newspapers, including a suburban weekly in Jackson, the state capital.

But she earned the enmity of Holmes County officials. In 1946 she was found guilty of contempt of court for interviewing the widow of a black who had been whipped to death. In 1954 she protested against the sheriff's brutality including his unprovoked shooting of a black man for allegedly "whooping" too loudly. The sheriff sued her for libel and a jury awarded him $10,000, but the Mississippi Supreme Court overturned the judgment - affirming that Smith had done nothing except print true facts.

83

After the U.S. Supreme Court outlawed school desegregation that same year, a White Citizens' Council was organized in Holmes County to subvert the law by using economic and social pressure to maintain segregation. Smith refused to support the organization. When a white man wounded a black school teacher because she complained when he damaged her yard, Smith printed the story. After the White Citizens' Council forced a doctor, minister, and farm operator to leave the county (and state) for believing in integration, she fought on their behalf.

She won award after award for her courageous stands - from the National Federation of Press Women, Women in Communications, the International Society of Weekly Newspaper Editors, the National Editorial Association and the Mississippi Press Association among other groups - but she was nearly put out of business. First the Council caused her husband to lose his job as administrator of the local hospital. Then in 1958 her opponents started a new weekly newspaper in Lexington, subsidized by well-to-do Council supporters, solely to take advertising away from her and drive her out of the county. An advertising boycott, which continued for 17 years, was organized against her newspapers and the printing plant for her suburban weekly in Jackson was bombed. Racists burned a cross on her lawn and spread vicious rumors and threats.

Still she refused to give in and struggled on borrowed money to keep publishing so she could give the public the truth. In a county where 19,000 blacks outnumbered whites three to one, she was a lonely voice insisting that the law should be colorblind.

"Even if I was just one white person, I was a beacon of hope to thousands of people," she recalled. "They looked on me as a symbol of hope and I was one white person who stood up for what was right."

In 1964, Smith, whose four weeklies had a combined circulation of 10,000, received the Pulitzer prize for excellence in editorial writing. The award was based on her work during 1963 when she protested the unprovoked slaying of a black World War II veteran by police and condemned the arrest of a black on trumped-up charges of firebombing his own home after he attempted to register to vote.

The slaying victim, Alfred Brown, a mental patient, was shot in the back by a policeman who attempted to arrest him on a false charge of suspicion of being drunk. The killing occurred just four days before the murder of Medgar Evers, a black civil rights leader in Jackson. When law authorities refused to give her any information about the Brown slaying, Smith drew on her wide acquaintance in the community to piece together the facts presented in a news story and deplored in an accompanying front page editorial in the Lexington Advertiser. The two Lexington policemen named in the slaying story filed a $100,000 libel suit against Smith which was eventually dropped.

In covering the firebombing incident, ignored by the White Citizens' Council newspaper, Smith again gave the facts in news stories and expressed her moral outrage in accompanying editorials. Proclaiming that a "lying editor" is "no good," she also commented editorially on her role in a suit brought by the U.S. Justice Department against the Holmes

County sheriff for civil rights violations. During the case she testified that she had heard the sheriff say, "I do not intend that any Negro will vote while I am sheriff." Defending her testimony in the face of accusations from the White Citizens' Council newspaper that she had lied, Smith said, "Every one of us should be willing to stand up and be counted for what is right."

Born in Gadsden, Alabama, in 1914, Smith started her career by writing "personal" items for a nickel-an-inch for her hometown paper before attending the University of Alabama.

As a journalism student, she told the acting president of the University of Alabama that she was determined to be her own boss. "I told him, I don't plan to take dictation when I finish college, I plan to give it," she said. "I've been liberated all my life...."

Smith has been a member of the Mississippi Council of Human Relations, an adviser to the U.S. Civil Rights Commission, secretary of the Holmes County Democratic Committee and a delegate to the Democratic National Convention.

She was named Woman of Conscience by the National Council of Women of the U.S. in 1964 and was recipient of the Lovejoy award from the University of Southern Illinois in 1960. A past president of the Mississippi Press Association, Smith remains in the newspaper publishing business in Holmes County. She and her husband, Walter D., live in Lexington, Mississippi.

SMITH INTERVIEW

Question: Can you tell us what you did that summer of 1963, when you heard about the killing of the Lexington black? How did you go out and report that story?

Smith: Well, the first thing that I did was to find out the man's name and, of course, I couldn't get any information from the local law officials in the city of Lexington. This happened on one of the main streets in the town, a business street, a block down from my office. A block that is predominantly black.... So, of course, the first thing I did was to inquire in the black community to find out which Brown it was.

Question: How did you identify him?

Smith: Someone in the black community told me he was such and such a Brown and he lived in such and such a place. Well, I telephoned around to the Browns until I found the right family and identified him for certain.... That's the way you gather news in a small town, particularly in something you know that's controversial.... It was the only way because usually at that time the law wouldn't even talk to you about anything like that because they didn't want you to write about it--the sheriffs and the town marshals. As a matter of fact, I got the story about what happened from...eyewitnesses, people who...saw the thing happen.

Question: How did you locate them?

Smith: By just keeping on talking to people and somebody would say "I think so and so was in that crowd" and you just keep on and on. It happened on a Saturday night, I had about three days on it. That's one thing about running a weekly, you know, you don't usually have to meet a deadline that afternoon and so I had time to investigate and find out who it was and I got the truth about what happened. I got it from eyewitnesses and I was sure I had the truth so I...printed the story. Of course, I tried to get the officers to make a statement but they...wouldn't. But then what they did do after I had printed the story? They each entered a lawsuit for $50,000 against me. Well, I verified what I had heard. What I had heard was that he (the victim) wore a white bracelet which identified him as having been in an institution...of some kind, like a hospital...and I verified...that he was wearing this when he was shot.... Everything that I wrote was the verified facts.

Question: Do you have any idea of how many people you talked to before you tracked down the facts in this Alfred Brown slaying?

Smith: It might have been 25 or 30, easily.

Question: And you were satisfied you had the correct information even though the law enforcement people wouldn't tell you anything?

Smith: Right. Then I wrote the story and I printed it and of course the thing about it is that people in my county really and truly...don't approve of violence like that. And, of course, it made the officers just look awful,...because it WAS awful. It was an awful thing they did...it could have been avoided. Completely. And, so the thing about it is...the people reacted. I wasn't trying to incite the population, you know. I wrote a very low-key factual story...and my memory of it is that I also wrote something in my column condemning the action. I mean, I always condemned violence.... I mean, when the officers of the law who are sworn to uphold the law lose their respect for the law to the extent that they become lawless themselves, well, then I criticize them because...it's their responsibility to uphold the law and to make other people respect the law. Well then they have to respect it themselves and so the outcome of that was that both of those men entered identical $50,000 law suits against me for alleged libel, but then we wore it out in the court. But, anyway, these men did not want this case to come to trial and my memory of it now is that they just kept postponing it from one court (date) to the other.

Smith: ...a friend of mine, a man that I had been close to...called me and said, "Hazel...what are you trying to do, start a riot?" And you know...it just really ran through me that here he could have so little understanding. And I said, "Hell, no, I'm not trying to start a riot. I'm trying to stop one." And, I was really furious, that he called me and criticized me for running that story. But you see, my philosophy,...is that I don't have the right to withhold the story when the local law officials who are supposed to uphold the law take the law into their own hands and kill somebody...without provocation. I don't have the right to withhold a story like that from my readers even if I wanted to....

Question: Do you recall the next incident in which the home of a black man, Turnbow, was bombed after he tried to register to vote?

Smith: I remember very distinctly about that. A white man from over in the Delta section of Holmes County...heard about the shooting and called me to tell me about it . I had interviewed Turnbow at the court house; he was the first person to go into the office of the circuit clerk in Holmes County in Lexington to register to vote.... So when I heard his house had been firebombed, well, my husband and I went over to his house and took pictures of the place. He had a nice little home and he had done all this work on his house himself and then of course they were saying that he fired it himself, when any fool would know that a man doesn't work there for months and months, screening the front porch and putting steps in and all that and then turn around and burn his own house.

Question: Was this story something that the authorities wanted to suppress?

Smith: They would have preferred that it not be written but we went over and took the pictures and we ran the pictures on the front page of the paper.

Question: If you hadn't done this reporting would people have known what was going on?

Smith: No, the white people would have never known about it. Only the black people in the community would have known about it. Because of it, their fear of the law would have been just that much worse and their alienation from the white community would have been just that more complete and they would have been just that much more frustrated and unhappy with their lot and resentful and bitter and eventually they would have learned to hate completely.

Question: These were things that were never reported by the other local newspaper?

Smith: No, not by the newspaper that was established in late '58 or '59 for the express purpose of putting me out of business. They tried everything for three years to put me out of business and couldn't do it.

Question: This was because you originally told a local group of prominent citizens that you intended to write about their establishment of the White Citizens' Council?

Smith: I said you can't keep anything like that quiet. There's no way. I said if you must have this organization, and I see no reason for it, then don't make it secret. Let the people know who's in it. Let them know that you're in it. Let them know that other white leaders in the community are in it and then the black people will not be scared of it because they wouldn't think that you would be engaging in any type of violence. And that was absolutely true at that time.

Question: How did you feel about Supreme Court decision in '54 to integrate the public schools? Were you for it?

Smith: No, I wasn't for it and I wasn't against it. I recognized that forced segregation creates an inherently unequal situation.

Question: Why did the community group set up this White Citizens' Council?

Smith: This was what was called the massive resistance plan to the Supreme Court decision. It was the white South's answer to what it considered forced integration of the races and, of course, their belief at that time, and some of them may still believe that way for all I know, was that school integration would be followed by social contacts and marriage and the amalgamation of the races and what have you, you know, and the thought of Negro blood in white veins was repugnant and horrible to them. And they thought the only way they could keep that from happening was to prevent integration of the schools.

Question: How did that strike you?

Smith: Well, I thought this, I thought that their fears were really groundless...marriage is such a personal thing and a person ought to have the right to marry whoever they want to marry. And what I thought they were going to do was to disrupt the peaceful relations that we had there—maybe we mistook them for being good race relations—but at least they were peaceful. I felt like the White Citizens' Council would destroy that and it did completely. Then fear took over and you see when people are afraid, well, anything can happen.

Question: So you wrote immediately then about the formation of the White Citizens' Council and about its stand?

Smith: Oh, you could not go into what their stand was because they weren't letting the people know what they stood for. It was just that they were standing to preserve "their way of life" is the way they put it and that could mean anything. But to the knowing people it meant preserving segregation in all of its forms. The White Citizens' Council was saying that you don't have to integrate, all you have to do is just stand up and say you're not going to integrate your schools and the federal government cannot force you. The Citizens' Council was not telling the people the truth. I just made a statement that when it came to a court test then it would be a question of the law. That in the event of a court suit, then the schools would be integrated and that we would be forced then with a decision of whether or not to obey the law and then we would be on the wrong side of the law. Again, that's printing the truth and the people don't want to hear it.

Question: And it was in the middle fifties when you said this over and over again?

Smith: In '56 and '57, all along for three or four years.

Question: And then events peaked at the culmination of the murder of Brown and the firebombing of Turnbow's house?

Smith: The firebombing of Turnbow's house, that marked the first effort to register voters in Holmes County - black voters.

Smith: They were trying to get into the system. They were trying to get in and be a part of it and to me that was the great tragedy that the white people could not see. They saw the black man and his vote only as threat, knowing that they were outnumbered three to one, they saw the blacks taking over the county completely, you see. That's what they thought and they were afraid of that and they didn't want that and they were fighting for what they thought was survival. I could understand why they did it, but I could also see that if they fought against it hard enough, they would engender enough bitterness and enough strife to where it was going to come anyway. The black man was going to get that vote and if in the interim they (the whites) acted so badly that they earned the undying hatred of the blacks, then there could never be an accommodation between the blacks and whites in the county and the county would, in fact, eventually become all black as they feared.

WRITING SAMPLES:

SMITH

SENSELESS KILLING

(Editorial)

Many Lexington citizens have expressed concern and regret that a 38-year-old Negro war veteran was shot and killed in our community Saturday night by city policemen.

From all accounts of reliable eye witnesses, the killing was senseless and could have been avoided by officers who either knew or cared what they were doing.

In these days of high tension and widespread racial strife, it would appear that officers sworn to uphold the law and protect all of the people would make a special effort to discharge their duties cooly and without bias; that they would go the extra mile to avoid giving even the appearance of oppressing any citizen of whatever color or status.

No person blames an officer for defending himself when his life is threatened by a criminal when he is in real danger. We do not believe in coddling criminals or law breakers in any fashion. But such was clearly not the case on Saturday night.

The victim was a harmless sick man who had never been in trouble his whole life with anyone, a man who had served our country honorably in the armed forces. His natural resentment of an unprovoked arrest on a false and baseless charge, his instantaneous fear of being locked up in the Holmes county jail, was and is understandable.

If we are to continue to have racial peace here, the present situation needs a great deal of improvement from the standpoint of law enforcement--and spirit and attitude as well. Officers guilty of lawless or unbecoming conduct should be made to give an accounting of their actions, the same as ordinary citizens.

An honest and complete investigation should be made by competent authorities - and no whitewash attempted.

And officers should be ordered to treat with respect and dignity all people with whom they come in contact.

June 13, 1963

Hazel Brannon Smith
94

DO MISSISSIPPIANS TODAY, AS SIR WINSTON [CHURCHILL]
PUT IT SO BEAUTIFULLY, HAVE THE HABIT OF LIBERTY?

(Editorial)

There was a time, almost a decade ago, when we Mississippians were free...we did have the habit of liberty. Newspaper editors were free to write editorially about anything in the world, giving our honest opinions, and there was no fear of economic reprisals or boycott. Today a newspaper editor thinks a long time before he writes anything that can be construed as controversial....

The editor of this newspaper has opposed the racist Citizens' Council from the very beginning--not because we oppose racial integrity and constitutional government they now claim to foster--but because in 1954 we recognized it as a serious threat to the personal freedom, peace and security of every living Mississippian--and its potential as a real Gestapo to take over the state. It is the individual freedom of our friends and readers we have and are fighting for....

Our personal opposition to the Citizen's Council (although we have a large number of personal friends who belong to it) has been vindicated time after time in the past nine years as one after another good Mississippian has been smeared, lied about and given Citizen's Council treatment--many of them now living in other communities or in other states.

That we have survived at all is a miracle we attribute only to God--but if He is for us then it makes no difference who is against us.

God willing, we shall endure

June 20, 1963

Hazel Brannon Smith

ARREST OF BOMBING VICTIM IS GRAVE DISSERVICE

(Editorial)

It is not moral or just that any man should live in fear, or be compelled to sleep with a loaded gun by his bedside.

Holmes County Deputy Sheriff Andrew P. Smith's action in arresting a 58-year-old Negro farmer, Hartman Turnbow, for firebombing his own home has come as a numbing shock to the people of Holmes County.

It is a grave disservice to our country and all our people in these days of increasing racial tension and strife. White and Negro citizens of Holmes county alike simply could not believe that something like this could happen in our country, that a man and his wife and 16-year-old daughter could be routed from sleep in the small hours of the morning and be forced to flee their homes literally in terror, only to be shot at by intruders outside - then to have the head of the family jailed the same day for doing the dastardly deed by an officer sworn to uphold the law and protect all citizens.

The only evidence presented against the aged Negro man at the preliminary hearing was only an account of the bombing and shooting incident as reported by Turnbow.... Mr. Smith added his own opinions and supposition as did county Atty. Pat M. Barrett who prosecuted the case. As a result the man was bound over under $500 bond for action by the Holmes County Grand Jury in October.

....Four other Negroes who had been arrested the same day in connection with the same case were released for lack of evidence. Not one shred of evidence was presented for them. But they had been held in jail five days and five nights.

....We have always taken pride in being able to manage our affairs ourselves. When we become derelict in our duty, and do not faithfully execute our obligations, we may rest assured it will be done for us. FBI agents and U.S. Justice officials have already made an exhaustive investigation of this bombing and shooting incident.

May 16, 1963

Hazel Brannon Smith

...the click of a box.

JOHN R. HARRISON
Gainesville (Fla.) Sun
Pulitzer Prize—Editorial Writing
1965

7

For most community newspapers the winning of one Pulitzer prize represents the zenith of achievement. But to the Gainesville (Fla.) Sun (circulation 28,100), the honor has come twice in less than a decade. Formerly owned by Cowles Communications Inc., the Gainesville Sun was purchased in 1971 by the New York Times.

In 1965 John R. Harrison, publisher, won a Pulitzer for a month's series of editorials that led to passage of the city minimum housing code which civic groups had been seeking unsuccessfully for years. Six years later Horance G. Davis, Jr. (see Page) received the same prize for editorials that helped to calm community fears after a sudden court order calling for immediate school desegregation.

A city of about 65,000 residents in north Florida, Gainesville, the home of the University of Florida, represents a cross-spectrum of Southern society from college professors to unemployed laborers. About 20 per cent of the city is black. Calling attention to the city's reputation as a progressive center of learning, Harrison pointed out the irony of a substantial number of citizens deprived of dignity and equal rights.

Harrison now is president of the New York Times Affiliated Newspaper Group that owns 13 community newspapers in the South. He also is a vice-president of the Times Company and a director of the International Herald Tribune, Paris. Active in civic affairs and philanthropy, he has been on the board of directors of hospitals, educational institutions and community agencies in Florida. He now lives in Lakeland, Florida, with his wife, Lois, and four children.

Born in 1933 in Des Moines, Iowa, Harrison was graduated from Phillips Exeter Academy and Harvard College. He also attended the Harvard Graduate School of Business Administration.

Becoming a New York Times executive when the Cowles chain was absorbed by the Times, Harrison attributes his success in part to marrying the daughter of his boss, Gardner Cowles (former president of the Des Moines Register).

"He gave me very close counselling over the years," Harrison said. "The real advantage in the beginning of my career was exposure to my father-in-law."

In writing his Pulitzer-winning editorials, Harrison used several techniques including his own reporting to get the facts. He personalized the series by making it a direct refutation of a statement from the mayor that a minimum housing code was unnecessary. His editorials, written in terse prose and accompanied by photographs, told the story of the people who lived in shacks and shanties.

Harrison also has won two Sigma Delta Chi Bronze Medallions for editorial writing plus a national Headliners Award and a Scripps-Howard Foundation/Walker Stone award for editiorial writing. The awards were for editorials calling for better treatment of migrants, competitive bidding on state engineering projects, and child care legislation.

HARRISON INTERVIEW

Question: How did you happen to move to Gainesville?

Harrison: The <u>Gainesville Sun</u> was purchased October 1, 1962, by Cowles Communications, a broadly-based communications company, the flagship of which was <u>Look</u> magazine.   It also published <u>Family Circle</u> magazine, <u>Adventure</u> Magazine.   They were in book publishing--they were in broadcast, television properties in Memphis, Des Moines, Iowa, and Daytona Beach, Orlando, Florida.   They had three small newspapers at that time in Gainesville, Florida, Lakeland, Florida, and Ocala, Florida.   The same family, the Cowles family, owned the <u>Des Moines Register Tribune</u>, the <u>Minneapolis Star Tribune</u>.

Harrison: I like to remember...and never forget...that fairly early in my career...I think I was 31...I become a vice president of Cowles Communications, and I gave a little talk to some journalism students at Gainesville.   And when I got finished, a young lady came up to me and she said, "You're pretty young to be a vice president of Cowles."   A journalism student, she said, "how did you do this?"   And I said, "I think it's a two-part formula.   The first part of the formula was that I went to work for Cowles Communications, Inc., and the second part of the formula," and I told her this was the part not to forget, "that I had the determination, perseverance, and the wisdom to marry Gardner Cowles' daughter."   She said she understood....   At any rate, I moved to Gainesville when Mr. Cowles purchased the paper; I was working for him at

the time.   When I came into Gainesville...well, I'd been there three
years before I wrote this particular series of editorials...and a builder
named Phil Emmer came to me one day and said that Gainesville, a
presumably enlightened city in central Florida, home of the University of
Florida, the largest educational institution in the state, had no minimum
housing code.   And Emmer was building--trying to build--low-cost housing
for the poor and the indigent, principally the black.   And he said that
the community needed the help of the newspaper to understand the problem
of trying to get the minimum housing codes, which in turn would trigger
urban renewal funds.   He made it very clear that without a minimum
housing code it was law that you could not get urban renewal funds....
So I went with Emmer for several days, I can't remember how many...and
toured some of the black housing in the city of Gainesville.   Twenty per
cent of the homes in the community were black homes.   I was literally
shocked.

Question: You were a reporter at this time?

Harrison: No, I was the president and publisher.   It brings up an
interesting point...I really went into newspapers because I liked to
write, one, sparked by the interest of a particular English teacher at
Exeter, and then I think further by a marvelously enriching experience at
Harvard College.

Harrison: But any rate, with that background, writing and use of the
language became very important to me.   My father-in-law influenced me to
go into small newspapers.   He was in the Des Moines and Minneapolis
papers and magazines at that time; and he felt the wave of the future in
America was...the small newspaper business.   I remember a quote almost
verbatim from William Butler Yeats: He said writing...precise writing,
is really just a constant series of rewriting.   And you rewrite until it
comes right like the click of a box, and then you know you have it.
Well, that kind of reading I'm sure had an influence on any eventual
writing that I did.

Harrison: So then I got to Gainesville and, taking over a new
property, I'm sure I didn't write for a while because of time demands.
And it was a public company and my father-in-law was a terribly demanding
task-master.   Probably most of what I learned in the newspaper business I
learned from Mr. Cowles.   So I concentrated very hard on the fiscal
side--business side--of the paper for a while, and then got into some
writing, oh, on selected topics.   I can't write about something unless I
feel very strongly about it.   That's why it almost embarrasses me that I
would win some of these writing awards when people like the editorial
writer in the office next door...he writes beautifully....   And, in my
opinion, doesn't get the deserved recognition that he should get.   Those
are the unsung heroes of the small newspaper business.

Question: What is your title now?

Harrison: Oh, I've got a whole batch of fancy titles...I'm vice
president of the New York Times and Company, and vice president of the
New York Times Media Company, which is a broad-based holding company, and
a director of the New York Times Media Company, which again is the
holding company of all the subsidiaries, broadcast magazines, book

publishing, newspapers, small newspapers. And the Times owns 13 small
newspapers in South. There are ten in Florida and three in North
Carolina, and I'm president of each of these corporations, but we hide
that.... We don't want people in the communities to know that because we
think that hometown journalism is most effectively practiced by the
publisher and the editor in the community.

Question: So you've been working for the Times since '71 (when
Cowles Communications sold out to the Times)?

Harrison: Right.

Question: When you saw these houses in Gainesville and they were in
such deplorable shape, did you come back and immediately launch a
campaign to try to get this minimum housing code through, or was it much
more difficult than launching a campaign?

Harrison: It was a simple problem. As late as August 5, 1964, the
mayor of Gainesville, he was a friend of mine named Howard McKinney, was
saying "A minimum housing code is unnecessary."

Harrison: I went back after I toured all this housing and I did
research in the morgue...and I use the term loosely, because small
newspapers don't have much of a morgue. I was able to determine that
documented studies by the League of Women Voters and other interested
groups in the community had shown that 21.9 per cent of the houses in the
city limits of Gainesville were classified as dilapidated or
deteriorating.

Question: Why didn't you assign a reporter or editorial writer to do
this? Why did you, the publisher, do it?

Harrison: I think I became passionately interested in what Emmer had
told me when he came into my office. He didn't go to a reporter or an
editorial writer. You know, in a small paper, the public thinks of...the
guy who runs the paper as THE guy...they don't know what else I do.
Hell, in this community (Lakeland) I get calls from people who are mad
because they didn't get their paper delivered. My lawyers like to kid
me, we were in a negotiating session one day and some fellow said he had
to talk to me. And I had to leave the session...this was in
Gainesville...and I left the conference room, and went to my office, and
the fellow was a man who didn't know me, but I was the publisher of the
paper and listed in the masthead, and he said that the paper had left out
the Cedar Key tides that day and he wanted to know what the tides were.
So I had to go get the tide chart and bring it back and read it to him.
My lawyers never let me forget that. But people don't...including my
lawyers...understand that that is hometown journalism and that is what
it's all about. It's like Letters to the Editor. I watch very carefully
the Letters to the Editor that come into the paper and how the paper's
responding to them and what the paper's doing about them. To me that's
the thrill of hometown journalism...that if you do feel strongly about
social issues, if you're in a hometown newspaper, you have opportunity
within time limits to get involved. You may not be able to do it every
day or every week, but you may be able to do it three or four or five, or
once or twice each year, or 15 times a year, if time permits. That to me

is the thrill of what you can do in hometown publishing, the dialogue you have with the audience, the closeness you have with your audience.

Harrison: It goes back to a philosophy of my father-in-law, that he always felt, still does, that the small hometown newspaper has the opportunity to have a much greater impact on its audience than the New York Times or the Des Moines Register-Tribune or the Minneapolis Star-Tribune. They (small newspapers) have a much greater opportunity because of the audience.... First of all, so many of them are your customers. They have a kind of proprietary interest in their hometown, it's their paper. Many of them...you'd be amazed, absolutely amazed, how many letters to the editor...refer to it as our paper, our newspaper, I'm ashamed that my newspaper took this position...the possessive pronoun is used very freely by people. I can't even remember reading a letter to the editor in the New York Times saying my newspaper. Does that answer your question?

Question: Yes, that certainly does. So when the builder came to see you, you took up this cause?

Harrison: Yes. So then I did some research. I didn't ask anybody to do the research for me. I figured if I'm interested in what Emmer is talking about, and if there is something here that really needs to be corrected, then I'd better be the guy to go after it.

Question: You said you were shocked when you went out and saw the houses. What stood out in your mind about these dwellings?

Harrison: Well, I remember one home,...shack really is what it was. It was leased for $45 a week. I saw a man, a black man, who was eating some beans out of a pie tin. I had no idea that there was an area where there were whole blocks of homes like the one where this fellow lived, this old fellow...you had to walk two or three blocks to get water.... They had no running water in the house. They went to a spigot two or three blocks down the road, in the city limits of this enlightened center of science and education and medicine in Florida. That's the slogan of the City of Gainesville; it was just ironic.

Harrison: So there were no screens on the windows, no plumbing, no running water. Flies and roaches and bugs and all kind of things. The front door had been a screen door and there were no screens in the door, just the frame, the shell, of the door.

Harrison: I questioned the people who lived in the homes about their rent and how they paid it and they were very, very cautious; they were scared to death. You see, the slumlord typically in the South gets the tenant so far in debt to him that the tenant really can't say anything bad, because the fear is that the slumlord will take him into court to collect the back rents. And it's almost...I learned it doing that series...it's almost by design that the slumlord will let them get just a bit in debt and make sure they stay a bit in debt. It's almost like the old company town. There's no way out...because if the tenant acts up then the slumlord just sends the fellow out and says, "Now here's the court order we're going to use to evict you, and to get you into court to pay the back rent."

Harrison: So then I did the research and it confirmed the quantity dilapidated interior housing and that 35 per cent of the fire calls were in that area...35 per cent were in an area of less than 20 per cent of the homes, 84 per cent of the adult court convictions were in the area, 68 per cent of the mental disease, 63 per cent of the hookworm--I went to the Public Health Department to get some of this...58 per cent of the tuberculosis, 80 per cent of the first-grade children there had positive or doubtful tuberculin skin tests, 53 per cent of the juvenile delinquency was occurring in slightly less than 20 per cent of a given area of the community.

Harrison: So I went back in history...and I think this was important to what we were trying to do because it showed that it was a long struggle, it was not a spur-of-the moment struggle. Stories all the way back to '52, '57, '58, showed that for years Gainesville citizens had been working diligently trying to correct these conditions, but unsuccessfully. And early in 1964, ahead, way ahead of my writing, before the builder came to me, a minimum housing code had been drawn up and presented to the city commissioners and the mayor, and on August 5, 1964, the mayor announced that no housing code was necessary in Gainesville.

Question: Why was that? Because he owned some of the property?

Harrison: You ask a very pertinent question and I neglected to tell you, he was a realtor.

Question: And he did own some of them?

Harrison: No. No. ...he did not personally. In most Southern communities the realtors have always been very concerned about minimum housing codes if they trigger urban renewal funds because the realtors do not participate in leasing urban renewal projects, generally. There are some exceptions to that.

Harrison: And part of what is necessary to understand about the Gainesville editorials and some of the ones that we have here, and in small newspapers all over the South, and maybe elsewhere, but particularly in the South... that there is an economic super-structure that runs the community. And the philosophy is that I want you (the papers) to go along with what is right for the community, or if you don't, economically, I'll break your back. And sometimes they're very blatant about it. I mean, they'll boycott us, (newspapers) and not advertise with us, sue us, and do all kinds of things. Well, we found that in community after community you have to take that first tough stand, and go all the way, and maybe you have to take ten very difficult unpopular stands and go all the way, to convince the people who have been running the community that economic interest can be equally, if not more, important (on the side of change).

Question: Well, then, when you pursued the information...you referred to those previous stories....

104

Harrison: Oh, yes, sure. And then the first editorial came out on
November 20. You remember on August 5 I said that the mayor had said
there's no need for a minimum housing code. And the editorial
essentially just decried the blight of substandard housing in Gainesville
and called for a minimum housing code. And I described a little child I
saw who was walking two blocks carrying the water back to the house,
described the house a bit, and described the conditions in the house, and
referred to Emerson.... (See page 109.)

Harrison: The next editorial was commenting on a city commission
meeting (to consider) a 50-page proposed housing code, and officials got
through 18 pages and there was so much argument that they just gave up.

Harrison: The next editorial used a photojournalism technique. I
had a photographer go out and take some pictures.

Question: Interesting in editorials, that's unusual.

Harrison: And then I got into the moral purpose of the issue,
pleading for human dignity and the rights of man, but based on...sound
reasoning and unvarnished facts. And just reciting for the first time
the statistics about hookworm and tuberculosis and delinquency occurring
in this area. Again, that was research that I had to do.

Question: Apparently there was a lot of research that went into the
editorials that had never appeared in the news columns before?

Harrison: ...a philosophy of mine and my associates, is that too
many small newspapers are hung up about this idea that you have to keep
having an expanded and explained news peg for everything you say in an
editorial. And our philosophy is that you can use just the germ of a
news peg in a small paper, particularly in a small town....

Harrison: But a small newspaper simply doesn't have the resources
and the manpower to keep going back and describing over and over again
what the blighted housing is, and...how pervasive the health problems are
and how terrible the economic relationship between the landlord and the
tenant are, so our attitude has always been that you should take that one
news peg which we had here on August 5, (when the code was rejected) and
we'd had for ten years, and go out and look at it. My own feeling is
that I can't write about something that I don't really know and
understand and feel very strongly about. And so look at it, investigate
it, research it, do all kinds of background on it, and I think some
journalism people disagree with that.

Question: Yes, I think the old style was that the editorial had to
be a commentary on something that had already appeared in the news
columns, But as you say, that isn't always feasible, especially in the
community press.

Harrison: No, in the small paper you're not going to get very far
with that approach.

Question: In the Gainesville situation, what groups in town profited
from the lack of a minimum housing code...apparently the realtors stood

to gain nothing by the implementation of such a code, but what other groups were against it, and why?

Harrison: Well, anybody who was a developer or a realtor saw this...real or unreal...as a threat to low-cost housing that he would either build, develop, lease or sell.

Question: So the groups that owned this property obviously opposed the code. Did these groups retaliate in any way against the newspaper? Did they threaten to boycott the paper?

Harrison: No, they really didn't.   No, there was no threat of boycott. But, they got very angry.

Question: Did they come to see you, and declare you were leading the community....

Harrison: It seems to me they might have written some letters. And McKinney, the mayor, would call me a couple of times, and said, "You're getting pretty rough on me." I personalized it very much because I could hang it around him, and he said a minimum housing code isn't necessary; it became very personal. And I would see him in a social atmosphere. He was an owner of a bank and realtor and a developer, and he was quite a problem all the time, involved in the community...an insurance company, bank, real estate company, development company, he was involved in a lot of things. But, not a lot of contact, he might have called me once or twice and said, "You're getting pretty rough," and I said, "Yeah." And I said, "We're determined, and we're going to stay on until we get it."

Harrison: One story that the paper ran about the code when it passed described pretty well the opposition. The mayor still at the end voted against it. Here's the kind of thing one of the commissioners said, "A housing code would already have been passed if not for the continual sniping at it and us"...it means by what I was writing.

Question: Do you agree it would have been passed if the paper hadn't exposed all of it?

Harrison: No, I don't think so.

Question: Do you think that probably it would have come anyway, but that the paper's emphasis on this made it come several years before it would have gone through otherwise?

Harrison: I think that's hard to say. I think in most issues, in retrospect, you can look back and say, yes, they would probably have come anyway.

WRITING SAMPLES:

HARRISON

MEMO TO McKINNEY

(Editorial)

The road was dust, and the small Negro boy strained under the weight of the bucket he was carrying. He had brought it more than two blocks from the fountain that was provided 'as a courtesy,' the sign told us. Three to five times a week the child makes the trip.

That child lives in a house eighteen feet by twenty-four feet along with three other people.

On several of the open windows there are no screens.

There is no front door at all.

Sunlight comes through the roof in two places.

The child and his family share with another family the outhouse in the backyard.

Not only is there no lavatory in the house, there is no tub, shower or hot water supply.

The siding on the house had deteriorated, the chimney needed replacing, the foundation was out of level.

The water lapped over the side of the bucket as the child stepped up a concrete block into the house.

Now, Mayor McKinney, that's a third to a fifth of the family's weekly supply of water.

To drink.

And that family lives in the Northeast section, within the city limits, of Gainesville, Florida, and they pay $5 a week rent. That's Florida's "University City," Center of Science, Education and Medicine.

Now, tell us again, Mayor McKinney, as you have since last August, that a minimum housing code for Gainesville is unnecessary, Tell us again that you want more discussion of the minimum housing code as you did last week. After all, the League of Women Voters and the Citizens' Housing Association of Gainesville, Inc., have, since 1955, documented by studies housing in Gainesville that has no indoor plumbing or piped-in drinking wather.

That's ten years, Mr. Mayor.

But tell the child that carries the drinking water down that dusty road that the minimum housing code is unnecessary.

In our mind's eye we'll try to console him with Emerson--"The dice of God are always loaded. For everything you have missed, you have gained something else. The world, turn it how you will, balances itself...Every secret is told, every virtue rewarded, every wrong redressed, in silence and certainty."

November 20, 1964

John R. Harrison

McKINNEY, YOU TELL IT TO BEULAH

(Editorial)

Beulah told us that the well water was even alright for cooking--if you boiled it plenty--but all the drinking water for her household came from the city faucet out on NE 8th Avenue. Then, of course, that drinking water usually stood around for a couple of days. Can't get to the faucet every day.

"The City of Gainesville Minimum Housing Code. Section 1.2.1. The City Commission of the City of Gainesville finds: that premises exist within the city of Gainesville which are blighted because there exist thereon blighted buildings, or other structures, either occupied or unoccupied by human beings, such buildings, and structures are blighted because of faulty design or construction, or failure to keep them in proper state of repair, or lack of proper sanitary facilities, or lack of adequate lighting or ventilation, or inability to properly heat, or any combination of these factors resulting in such buildings or structures becoming so deteriorated or dilapidated, so neglected, so overcrowded with occupants, or so unsanitary as to jeopardize or be detrimental to the health, safety, morals or welfare of the people of this city...."

Now, McKinney, you tell Beulah that the minimum housing code is "unnecessary."

You'll have to tell her. She doesn't read.

Beulah leaned back in her porch chair and scraped the food from her plate. She confessed the worst part about the outdoor privy was not the cold of winter, it was when it rained too much, and the water on the lot didn't drain.

The City of Gainesville Minimum Housing Code. Section 8.2.2. Dwelling and dwelling units. Each dwelling unit shall contain not less than one (1) kitchen sink, one (1) bathroom lavatory basin, one (1) bathtub or shower bath, and one (1) flush water closet."

Now, McKinney, you explain carefully to Beulah that although she doesn't have any of these things in the house now, neither the sink nor the lavatory nor the bathtub nor the water closet, you tell her that they are "unnecessary."

"The City of Gainesville Minimum Housing Code. Section 3.3.3. All yards and premises shall be maintained so as to prevent the harborage or breeding of insects, rodents or vermin and yards and premises shall be sloped or graded to provide for the disposal of surface water and to prevent the accumulation of surface water."

Now, McKinney, you tell her that although that surface water at times accumulated and stands and seeps very close to that privy and to the outside well, you tell Beulah that the minumum housing code is "unnecessary."

110

Men come together in cities in order to live; they remain together in order to live the good life."

--ARISTOTLE

Beulah lives her life within the city of Gainesville.

Gainesville. That's Florida's "Beautiful University City."

December 2, 1964

John R. Harrison

HUMAN DIGNITY, MCKINNEY

(Editorial)

I believe in an America where every family can live in a decent home in a decent neighborhood--and where the water is clean and the air is pure...

JOHN F. KENNEDY

Come with us, Mayor McKinney, and visit the blighted areas of Gainesville, Florida.

Come with us and see a city that, on the one hand, boasts the second highest effective buying income per household in the state of Florida, and, on the other hand, tolerates 21.9 per cent of its houses in the city limits to be classified as "dilapidated or deteriorating" housing according to the 1960 United States Census.

Come with us, McKinney, and see substandard housing areas where the youngest child alive can, when he grows to manhood, judge us as a city by whether we made provisions just to have drinking water in that child's home.

Or indoor plumbing.

Or electricity.

Or heat.

Come with us and review the study made back in 1958 by the League of Women Voters and the Citizens Housing Association of Gainesville that revealed the following shocking conditions in substandard housing areas:

(1) 35 per cent of the city's residential fire calls were in the areas.

(2) 84 per cent of the adult court convictions were in the areas.

(3) 68 per cent of the mental disease.

(4) 63 per cent of the hookworm.

(5) 58 per cent of the tuberculosis.

(6) 80 per cent of the first grade children had positive or doubtful tuberculin skin tests.

(7) 53 per cent of the juvenile delinquency.

In areas where 21.9 per cent of the city's total housing units were classified as "dilapidated or deteriorating."

112

We think the vast majority of the alert and responsible people of Gainesville, dating back into the decade of the fifties, would disagree with you that "a minimum housing code is unnecessary."

They have a high regard for human dignity.

For a man's right to be able to rent a decent house.

To live in a safe and sanitary neighborhood.

To try to avoid hookworm.

And tuberculosis.

December 9, 1964

John R. Harrison

You've got to write to somebody.
Just words on paper are useless.

HORANCE G. DAVIS, JR.
Gainesville (Fla.) Sun
Pulitzer Prize—Editorial Writing
1971

8

Horance G. Davis, Jr. wrote his Pulitzer-prize-winning editorials for the Gainesville (Fla.) Sun against a background of community foot-dragging on school desegregation. Following the 1954 U.S. Supreme Court decision that banned school segregation, Gainesville, like many other communities, adopted a token plan but hoped to postpone complete desegregation as long as possible.

In January, 1970, the Alachua County school system, which includes Gainesville, was beginning preparations for a desegregation plan expected to go into operation the following September. The community was shocked when the U.S. Supreme Court ruled on January 15 that total school desegregation must take place by February 1. With integration an immediate reality, some residents followed the demagogic stance of Governor Claude R. Kirk and other politicians who vowed to challenge the court.

In his editorials Davis urged the community to follow the law and not give way to a "sickness of the soul." According to Ed Johnson, executive editor, The Sun measured the success of the campaign both by the actual school desegregation, which occurred on schedule, and the defeat of Kirk for re-election.

Davis is a professor of journalism at the University of Florida who practices what he teaches. In 1977 he was named a Distinguished Service Professor at the University where he earned both bachelor's and master's degrees. He and his wife, Marjorie, the parents of two children, live in Gainesville.

115

A former state capital correspondent for the <u>Florida Times-Union</u> of Jacksonville, Davis began teaching journalism at the University in 1954. While teaching, he has worked summers for the <u>Atlanta Constitution</u>, <u>Miami Herald</u> and other publications. Born in Georgia in 1924 and brought up in North Florida, Davis went to college on the GI Bill after serving as an Army Air Corp. lieutenant in World War II.

Refering to his family background of farmers and railroad workers, Davis said, "I guess I was only the fourth or fifth who got a college degree and I often say if it hadn't been for a little education, then I would have stayed over in north Florida and pumped Exxon gas and ridden with the Ku Klux Klan at night."

At the invitation of John R. Harrison, publisher of the <u>Sun</u>, (see page 97) Davis began writing editorials occasionally in 1962 and by 1967 was doing all of the paper's editorials while continuing to teach full-time. He did not become a salaried staff member, however, until after he won the Pulitzer.

"I might be the only Pulitzer prize winner who did anything on piece-time work," he said. "I was only getting about $17.50 to $20 an editorial. I think we had some agreement where I'd produce ten of them for $17.50 and to encourage my volume, i got $20 for any over ten."

Davis also has been honored for editorial writing by the Society for Professional Journalists, the Sidney Hillman Foundation, the American Bar Association and numerous other groups. His columns appear in the <u>Atlanta Journal-Constitution</u>.

DAVIS INTERVIEW

Question: Your editorials that won the prize were limited to the race situation on the local level, weren't they?

Davis: Sure, and incidentally, on editorial writing, I have a theory that all editorials ought to be local as much as they can be. When we were dealing with Vietnam, which we were opposed to beginning about 1967, I was very much aware that you couldn't very well localize all Vietnam editorials. Well, I grew tired of dropping this line in there - 36 local boys were killed in Vietnam, or 37, 38, 39, or 40. We got up to 44.   You can wear that out, ...so I'm well aware that all things cannot be localized. But, in this Pulitzer case,...we were acutely concerned with the local situation, particularly violence, and particularly fairness to whites and blacks.   It was an extremely explosive situation.

Question: This was in 1970?

Davis: I believe they gave us something like 17 days to accomplish massive integration of the schools.   Now, we had editorials pointing out that this really shouldn't have been any shock. Still, it was a shock because it had to be done overnight, and so quickly.

Question: Had any integration taken place during preceding years?

117

Davis: Well, it was freedom of choice, and that boils down to a few aggressive blacks placing their children in white schools; a few aggressive whites placing white children in black schools. And, in fact, we made fun of it back in the '60s. There was a memo I had in my files about the school superintendent saying that any children who wanted to (this was a freedom-of-choice plan trying to avoid court orders) go to a school of the opposite race could count on school officials getting them there if they had to bus them from kingdom come. So we used that quote later when the busing was compulsory, to point out how willing we were to do it under different circumstances.

Question: What position did your paper take?

Davis: Oh, the paper took the position that school integration reaped social benefit. And, in fact, the paper had been a pro-integration paper for years.

Question: Prior to its purchase by the <u>New York Times?</u>

Davis: Oh, yes. Oddly enough, I had reason to look over the editorials in 1967 and I didn't find any which said that the schools should not be integrated. That, it seemed, had not occurred to us. I think we were all pretty flabby and pretty satisfied with the way things were, and that was this freedom-of-choice kind of thing.

Question: What did your first editorial say? When you sat down to write this first editorial, what ideas went through your mind? What kind of preparation did you bring to the task?

Davis: Well, I think the first thing you recognize is the fundamental righteousness of the court decision and the sociological correctness of the thing. I think you start with that.... The second thing is knowing that you have community trouble coming. You try to head it off and temper it by lending what weight and authority the paper may have by first making it respectable - the court decision and everything - for after all, we had a Governor who didn't agree with this, and we had a strong Wallace depth in this section. So the thing to do first, once you recognize the sociological correctness of it, is to start calculating on how it can be accomplished without nuts and bolts. An editorial cannot put the "nuts and bolts" into it, the people have to do that, not editorials. So without putting nuts and bolts on it, how could you lend the paper's weight to this and accomplish it without extremes? I mean violence really is what we are talking about.

Question: What do you mean by "nuts and bolts?"

Davis: You cannot tell school officials the zones to pick, or how many kids to bus--we stay out of those nuts and bolts things. We elect and hire people to do those things and they...are more expert than we are.

Question: You mean professional school administrators in this case?

Davis: Sure. You don't put nuts and bolts in your editorial. It's gonna be unread, it's gonna be unlistened to and you are going to make mistakes and people are going to say "he's silly." So all you can do is put a big picture, big tone and that's what we were concerned with - tone....

Question: How big is Gainesville, and how was the community divided along racial lines, residential patterns, in 1970?

Davis: In 1970, the population was about 104,000. It's 135,000 now (1977). I mean this is the entire community, the entire county....

Question: And you have a county-wide school system?

Davis: County-wide, one-district school system. A consolidated school system. The district and the county are the same and the oddity is, like many Southern towns, a third of our school kids are black, but only 20 per cent or 18 per cent adults are black. The number of blacks has declined because of the economic opportunity. So what happens, we raise them, we are a nursery for the blacks. That's what it amounts to and then they go to the cities. Well, anyway, what it really boiled down was why not go ahead and integrate totally and truly 33 per cent blacks in every school.

Question: We spoke of the feeling in the back of your mind when you sat down to write these editorials, that you had an obligation to ward off violence. What made you think that violence might be?

Davis: Well, first of all, you had inflammatory statements printed in the news, as threats.

Question: You mean your paper ran them in news columns?

Davis: Threats! Sure, and letters and I guess we had a sense of feel for the community. You could sense about violence. And, then we had a startling development. You know, we whites form certain concepts,...and stick with them. And, here this suit had been pending all these years and led by a very respected black man, locally, Reverend T.A. Wright.... (We thought) that all the blacks wanted to do was go to school with whites, right? That's what it was all about, right? Same system. That's what we thought. And then, bingo, it turns out that that ain't the way it's supposed to be. The blacks don't want to be absorbed in this fashion.

Question: They wanted some of the whites in their schools?

Davis: Yeah, and they would just as soon be the majority. It turned out that we thought one-third was a perfect solution, but one-third turns out not to be the solution in terms of the black community, and then the school board did heap insults on injuries by closing the leading black high school.

Question: So there was violence then?

Davis: Oh yes. Nobody got killed, but we had vandalism, we had tear gas, we had roving gangs with bicycle chains.

Question: Who were they beating up?

Davis: A couple of blacks would beat whites and every once in a while whites would beat blacks, and we lauded certain strict rules. I think a 16-year-old black pulled a knife on a kid on the school bus and robbed him of his lunch money, and the judge gave him six years. It just couldn't be tolerated, and we just weren't going to have that kind of system, period. If it took six years in prison to stop it, fine. But, basically, the idea was to cool the whole business and help people get along together.

Question: The integration furor must have gone on for a considerble period of time?

Davis: It extended all year. There were editorials stimulated by news stories that when school reopened in September there was going to be more trouble, and some of the types around here, the law-enforcement types, laid down the rules as to what the law said about vandalism and violence and there were editorials laying it down to the kids that if you do any stuff you're going to catch it. In other words, this was an effort to put the fear of law into them, into the parents, too, that they were responsible for their kids' conduct. We have a state law to that effect, so we tried to curb violence when the school opened. We still had some sporadic violence after that.

Question: Did the school integration plan then require that more of the busing burden fall on the blacks than on the whites?

Davis: Percentage-wise, probably not, but...let's take this book that my students put out in my editorial writing class.

Question: It appears to be a book of material that your students prepared, but could you describe it?

Davis: The first three weeks of my editorial writing class are devoted to trying to get the students acquainted with the local community because they are going to write to that local community and each one of them is assigned a chapter and each class produces the book, and the subject matter - well the introductory letter says - "This book of facts about Gainesville's Alachua County in the State of Florida was compiled by students registered in the Public Opinion Class, College of Journalism and Communications, University of Florida. It is designed to be a profile of the community insofar as it can be compiled in a brief span of two weeks.... In total, however, it should be of value to any person desiring immersion in the community, especially those engaged in writing and gathering the news and commenting on daily events."

Davis: Now, you see, you're asking me how I knew a couple of things that I knew about violence and so forth. Well, here it is. This is a student of mine gathering this data, and here I am editing it, you see, as this thing is breaking. So that's why I know. Street talk. Black City Commissioner Neal Butler agreed a mid-year transfer would create a problem where the "conditions would have to get worse before getting better." He said the black community was tired of hearing "give us a little more time."

Question: Obviously, you think an editorial writer has to be immersed in the community?

Davis: I sure do. Now, here are two paragraphs in the fall 1970 book, dealing with events that we are talking about. Integration in the Alachua County schools - A Federal Court order ordered that this county comply with the February 1 desegregation order. This meant a sudden and massive integration of black and white students instead of the gradual change previously planned for Alachua county. The black high school, Lincoln, was closed down and these students put into Gainesville High School. This was done despite protests from Lincoln students who staged protest marches and even boycotted classes for several days. The integration seemed to go smoothly until March 26, 1970, when white students, 30 or more, raised the Confederate flag atop GHS victory pole. This was the beginning of open hostility between black and white students. The classes were so disrupted by this clash that school had to be called off once. Some students, considered trouble makers, were expelled or suspended. A special school on 39th Avenue was opened to take these students.

Question: Did you express a position on the opening of that school?

Davis: Yes, Hilltop or whatever the name of that school was, was designed to pull out white or black kids who simply just could not adjust to regular school.... I mean their mommy and daddy brought them there, and it was small--ten or twelve kids, and they were educated in all that was necessary in that environment, isolated from the general school system until they calmed down.

Question: This was a rather novel way of handling the situation, I think. Something that your paper campaigned for?

Davis: We didn't campaign for it, but we certainly supported it. I remember writing about the head of it - Dr. Russell Ramsey - and we knew him as a liberal type and he had headed the ROTC program here and kind of got out of the military because of Vietnam. He was a person that we thought acceptable for that kind of thing, and, well, I remember writing editorials in praise of him.

Question: Did you have complete information at hand when this order came through?

Davis: Yes.

Question: So it wasn't so difficult to sit down at the typewriter and attack the subject, was it?

Davis: No. Well, you know, you've got to know what you're doing in this business. Racial troubles interrupted the 1969-70 school year with three violent incidents after the transfer of the Lincoln High students. Quiet was restored after police patrolling and after parent-teacher groups and other citizen supporting groups helped smooth out most of the trouble.

Question: When was that, in the spring?

Davis: Yes, it was spring of '70. Then, okay, here we were back
to the violence. March 31 and April were marked by disruptions. Tommy
Thomas, administrative assistant to the superintendent of the schools,
commented, "It will still take some time before the remaining problems
will vanish. We didn't get into this mess overnight, and we won't get
out of it overnight." He felt that the problem was, "White parents not
adjusting to the situation, but that kids could work it out without
outside interference." Very perceptive. I think it was a good
observation. Parents were the problem. A surprising corps of opposition
developed among black educators who feared for their jobs in competition
with the whites. Now, we know that the fears were not idle speculation.

Question: Did you have any editorial comment on black opposition to
integration....?

Davis: Oh, yes, but put it this way, once you're committed on a
path, busing and integration in an editorial, you don't deviate much
because your deviation is seen as weakness by that segment that does not
want integration. So we have been die-hard busing even into an era when
I'm beginning to think it is not working like it should. Busing to
achieve the 70-30 percent black/white ratio described for the schools
involves about 1200 students. So now we bus almost almost 12,000
students (1977) of which only a tenth is for racial purposes. And this
is something we point out in editorials when anybody starts fussing about
busing because we are only busing a tenth of them for that purpose.

Question: What sort of advice do you give your students when they
begin writing editorials for you?

Davis: Well, the first thing that I tell them is that opinions
don't persuade, the facts do. Facts and events, and that rhetoric as
such, is useless. I make this analogy. I say, now you sit down and read
an editorial on highway safety or fastening your seat belts or whatever -
I say what the hell is that - but if you zip down the road and see an
auto wreck with a couple of bodies on the side of the road, what happens?
You drive more slowly, you drive safer for a while, don't you? So,
events and facts become primary, and so I make them do research. This is
the educational device that I use.... Also, I categorize editorials into
four types and I only permit them to write one of those types.

Question: What are the four types?

Davis: One is "Goody-Goody." This is the one in which you've got
to put balance into your editorial policy so that you won't always appear
negative. I've lived this. There are letters that appear in the paper
once in a while saying that you're always against things. I tell them
that editorial writing is like the white corpuscle system, it goes to
areas of infection. But anyway, the goody-goody is a balancing
situation. Another is the "Dear People," Dear people is a necessity
because it's what you do when you endorse candidates. There is no other
way if you're appealing to what I call the oatmeal mass and you're asking
them to stand up and walk and so the Dear People is a necessity because
of the circumstances. I mean, if you feel compelled to write a Memorial

Day editorial and you pick highway safety, that's a Dear People. I abhor them....

Davis: The next type is very important, I call it a posture editorial. You cannot guide an audience. It's a mistake - on a social issue - to wait until it has names and faces attached to it and people are throwing the bricks. The only way you can prepare a community for social change is to express faith in the system and say "this is America, this is the right way to do it," before it assumes personalities.... You prepare your community. Hell, call it anything you want but what you're doing is greasing the way for what you know is coming.

Davis: The last type I call the "action editorial." In an action editorial they must state a... problem of social significance, and go into great detail to try to analyze it. They must propose a concrete solution...it can't be calling for a study. It can't be just recommending putting money here unless they say where that money is going to come from.... They've gotta know who's got power to do what, and so that's the toughest to write and that's the kind I make them write. Then I give them a little bit about public opinion theory. This is the fact that in the power structure concept, the real people you are trying to reach are influential and the fact that influentials are stratified at various levels of society. One influential might not have any impact on another influential. It's a rather complicated concept...about how influentials operate and how they have screens if they reject your ideas - how you can get past the screen, that sort of thing....

Question: Then you don't think editorials are influential?

Davis: Right. Some people may call me an influential but I have no influence. How in the hell can I be an influential? Take some of these racial uprisings. We had arson. In fact all the white merchants have been burned down. How in the hell do you reach an arsonist? I remember thinking when I was writing one editorial that what I would like is for this to be written in such...beautiful, easy-to-understand language that ministers would read it from the pulpits. Maybe that would be my best chance of reaching somebody like them (arsonists).

Question: Because you thought these were not people who were arsonists ordinarily, but arsonists because of the pressures on them?

Davis: I used examples that just possibly might have some impact upon the arsonist. The example I used was a burned-out dry cleaner. A dry cleaner is awfully easy to burn-out and it was - the dry cleaner had been there thirty years - and the two white people that ran it had trained generations of black people to run dry cleaners and - in fact, they had about five or six people that had gone out and set up businesses. That's one point. The second point is that in Old Gainesville, it was a good dry cleaner and it was one of the few areas in the community that black and white culture came together - in this dry cleaners that was on the margin of the black area. So I used that as an example of how destructive this kind of thing could be from a sociological standpoint, in very simple language. Those are things you have to think about. You just don't write blind. You've got to think about who you're writing to. I don't think of them as a faceless mask. I don't have any hope of getting a faceless mask to do anything.

Question: So to whom were you writing?

Davis: I was writing to members of the black power structure, thinking if they knew an arsonist or some kookish guy who might be an arsonist that they would prevail upon him.

Question: On some of these hot-headed kids?

Davis: That's right. I had no idea that a hot-headed kid would pick up the Sun and would say, gee, they're addressing that to me, but it may be that if I could reach some segments of the black community, who knew a hot-headed kid in his house, he might say now, look, you calm down, look what this arsonist did down there. That's the way you're got to think. You've got to write to somebody. Just words on paper are worthless.

Davis: I don't believe you write editorials for winning awards. I don't do any writing for winning awards. That's the worst motive in the world.

WRITING SAMPLES:

DAVIS

GOODBYE, WILLIE LOMAN

(Editorial)

    Willie Loman was a beer-and-undershirt sort of guy who really wanted
to be something better, especially in the eyes of his son Biff, but he
couldn't quite make it. He wasn't humble about it, and he turned into a
loud-mouthed bore, trying to egg Biff on, until Biff said one day:

    "Pop! I'm a dime a dozen and so are you."

    And Willie's wife saw Willie's eyes film over and she cried in
desperation, "He's a human being and a terrible thing is happening to
him. Attention, attention must be finally paid to such a person."

    But is was too late, and Willie Loman left the house and committed
suicide.

    That's the way Arthur Miller tells it in his play, "Death of a
Salesman," and it turns out to be a pretty sad story about the fruits of
human neglect and callousness and selfishness and that final moment of
truth when a human being realizes the frigidity of his own soul.

    Did you feel the chill last Wednesday?

    Cloaked in the majesty of the law and with full thrust of moral
force, the U.S. Supreme Court singled out Alachua County by name and
declared that our school system is illegally contrived and we must
integrate the races.

    Not in ten years, not in five years, not in one year, but in 13
days.

    We can react with hysteria and jerk our kids out of school and make
threats and throw up quickie segregation academics. We can encourage the
kids to make trouble and the teachers to balk or quit. And we can tell
the School Board to go to jail rather than obey the law of the land.

    None of these things are likely to happen in Alachua County for a
very simple reason. We are not that kind of folk.

    In fact, the matter simply isn't that emotional to us. We were
peaceably integrated in 1965 and 27 per cent of our pupils already are
mixed and we already have taxed ourselves for school buildings needed for
full integration.

    In a way, the Supreme Court edict was like the bursting of a boil.
The indecision is over, the pressure is gone, and through the body

126

politic surges a wave of relief. The shadowy fear of the unknown was
dissipated last Wednesday, and now the task is plainly laid out. And we
are accustomed to tasks.

But in truth we are not ready--not physically ready--and there will
be much chaos in the next few months. Our children will be bussed to
strange schools and confront stranger teachers in strange surroundings
and brush against strange classmates, even classmates with strange caste
to their skins.

Black and white, we must not underestimate the confusion and
misunderstanding which confront us. But see the problem plainly. It is
a matter of sheer logistics--of moving bodies and books from one place to
another--and not a sickness of the soul.

A healthy soul is important. The main thing is the education of
our children, and it cannot be accomplished with a dead spirit and a
heavy hand.

The world is going to change for us all next February 1. We can
greet the new challenge with hope and enthusiasm. Or we can look into
the eyes of our children and see our failure mirrored there as Willie
Loman saw his failure reflected in the eyes of his son Biff.

"He's a human being and a terrible thing is happening to him," cried
out Willie Loman's wife as Willie left the house.

That is one heritage we will not leave.

January 18, 1970

Horance G. Davis, Jr.

THE MAGNOLIA EATERS

(Editorial)

Somebody wrote a play about Governor Lester Maddox of Georgia which expressed Maddox's high regard for "my white friends, regardless of race, color or creed."

Such magnolia eaters have been crawling out of the Florida woodwork in droves the past few weeks, ever since the federal courts clamped down on southern school segregation after 16 years of patient watchfulness.

True, the magnolia eaters have been notably silent these 16 years that racial integration has been the law of the land. But 1970 is an election year, a fact pointed enough to penetrate the dense matter between any politician's ears.

Perhaps the most hypocritical of all is Governor Claude Kirk. Three years ago he was loftily telling Alabama Governor Lurleen Wallace that he would not support her protest against integration because "Florida cannot join attempts to subvert or delay the law of the land as interpreted by the Supreme Court."

In the past two weeks, Governor Kirk has literally pounded open the doors of the U.S. Supreme Court twice in fruitless protests, jetted to numerous other federal courts to challenge integration, and issued executive orders contrary to court decisions.

Kirk, of course, is running for re-election.

Then there's State Sen. Tom Slade of Jacksonville who offered the U.S. Supreme Court his Mastercharge card to visit Florida and view the "chaos" personally. As protest, he also sent the court "the longest telegram in Western Union history."

Slade is running for state treasurer.

We must not overlook U.S. Rep. William C. Cramer of St. Petersburg, who sponsored a constitutional amendment to prohibit cross-busing of students. (Wouldn't that look great alongside the Bill of Rights?) But Cramer is a bit more consistent than others, because he first opposed busing in 1964.

Cramer is running for the U.S. Senate.

We wish we could report that common sense prevails otherwise among our state leaders but, sadly, it is not so. Efforts to thwart integration have been promoted recently by U.S. Congressmen Charles E. Bennett of Jacksonville, William C. Chappell of Ocala, Robert Sikes of Crestview, James Haley of Sarasota, Louis Frey Jr. of Winter Park and Herbert Burke of Hollywood.

That's a fine bunch of non-partisan magnolia eaters.

Not all of Florida's leadership has climbed aboard the streetcar named Desire. And the record should list them as heroes in the face of temptation.

State Education Commissioner Floyd Christian is seeking re-election, but he has shored up the educators from Perdido Bay to Key West. If law-and-order and justice come to prevail in the Florida school system, we will owe a vast debt to Christian.

Less credit goes to political hopefuls who have simply kept their mouths shut. Aspiring for the U.S. Senate are Fred Schultz and Farris Bryant of Jacksonville, along with Robert Haverfield of Miami. They have so far resisted racial opportunism. And so have gubernatorial aspirants Earl Faircloth of Tallahassee, Chuck Hall of Miami, Reubin Askew of Pensacola, and John Mathews of Jacksonville.

Florida once had a reputation for moderation in all things, including race. The pack of magnolia eaters, led by the master gobbler Claude Kirk, has destroyed that reputation with an orgy of political frivolity for personal gain.

There isn't a weight-watcher among the batch.

February 3,1970

Horance G. Davis, Jr.

FOR HOODLUMS ONLY

(Editorial)

This one is for young hoodlums.

Well, not exactly hoodlums. But if your household has a young rebel
with little respect for his fellows and a disregard for property rights,
who likes to make people squirm, has been known to twist arms, plays the
big shot role and generally likes to raise hell...if you have a youngster
like that in you household...

Clip this out and put it beside his supper plate.

Generally, we aim to communicate with readers and not speak for
them. But, today at least, we're convinced we speak for 99 per cent of
all Alachua Countians--including the moms and pops, the cops and the
judges, the teachers and the principals, the blacks and the whites.

The message: We will not condone hoodlumism in the public schools.

We had a touch of it last year. Some of it had a racial
connotation after integration on February 1. But it boiled down to
outright violent conduct--petty robbery in restrooms, beatings on the
parking lot, robbery on a school bus, even a minor riot or two.

Tragic as it was, one lad of 17 years drew a 15-year-prison
sentence. He took $6 at knifepoint.

His name was Izell Tyrone Booth. We do not think young Mr. Booth
should be an "example" of justice in Alachua County. Appropriately stiff
punishment should prevail in any future incident where the evidence
merits conviction--and it should fall equally upon white or black, old or
young.

And there is the matter called verbal violence--those little words
which make the blood run hot. And those nutty demonstrations, like
shouting down speakers and obscene salutes.

They cause trouble also.

Just so we understand each other, let's lay it on the table.

For those of you slightly rebellious and finding it hard to adjust,
there's Mountain Top School out at the juvenile shelter. A nice fellow
out there, Russell Ramsey, will keep you up on schoolwork and try to help
iron things out.

For those who persist, there is suspension and expulsion from
school. And for those who make that bad, bad mistake, the result is even
more unpleasant. Try these for size:

130

o Assault, five years imprisonment and $3,000 fine.

o Possession, use or concealment of a deadly weapon, up to five years imprisonment and $10,000 fine.

o Arson, up to 20 years imprisonment.

Please conclude from this that Alachua County WILL have peace in its schools this year. We WILL make safety havens of the campus. We WILL guarantee the welfare of our youngsters:

School opens next Monday.

So if you plan to make it a hot time on the old campus this year, take a piece of advice.

Don't.

September 11, 1970

Horance G. Davis, Jr.

The following is a list of Pulitzer prize winnners in public service, reporting, and editorial writing from the South (defined as the 11 Confederate states, omitting the border states of Kentucky, Maryland, Missouri and the District of Columbia). Asterisks denote those awards given in connection with stands on racial questions**.

Year	Winner	Category	Achievement
1923	*Memphis (Tenn.) Commercial Appeal	Public Service	Stand against Klu Klux Klan
1925	Charleston (S.C.) News & Courier	Editorial Writing	Call for new Southern political leadership
1926	*Columbus (Ga.) Enquirer-Sun	Public Service	Fight against Klu Klux Klan and lynching
1928	*Grover Cleveland Hall, Montgomery (Ala.) Advertiser	Editorial Writing	Stand against gangsterism and lynching
1929	*Louis Isaac Jaffe, Norfolk (Va.) Virginian-Pilot	Editorial Writing	Advocacy of legislation to prevent lynching
1931	Atlanta (Ga.) Constitution	Public Service	Exposure of municipal graft
1939	Miami (Fla.) Daily News	Public Service	Campaign for recall of the Miami City Commission
1946	*Hodding Carter, Delta (Greenville, Miss.) Democrat-Times	Editorial Writing	Editorials against racial, religious and economic intolerance

---

** Few prizes are given for one editorial or one news story. In most cases awards are made on the basis of a writer's work for an entire year, so pinpointing the exact subjects of award-winning achievements is difficult. Those listed have been taken from the two books by John Hohenberg, long-time secretary of the advisory board on the Pulitzer prizes - see Hohenberg, The Pulitzer Prize Story (1959) and The Pulitzer Prizes (1974), and - standard biographical sources on individual winners.

1948	George Goodwin, Atlanta (Ga.) Journal	Reporting	Exposure of vote fraud
1948	*Virginius Dabney, Richmond (Va.) Times-Dispatch	Editorial Writing	Stand against one-party system and poll tax; for racial moderation
1951	Miami (Fla.) Herald; Williams H. Fitzpatrick, New Orleans (La.) States	Public Service (Herald); Editorial Writing (Fitzpatrick)	Reporting of crime (Herald); analysis of constitutional issue (Fitzpatrick)
1953	*Whiteville (N.C.) News Reporter and *Tabor City (N.C.) Tribune	Public Service	Campaign against the Klu Klux Klan
1954	Vicksburg (Miss.) Post-Herald	Reporting	Coverage of a tornado
1955	Columbus (Ga.) Ledger and Sunday Ledger-Enquirer; Caro Brown, Alice (Tex.) Echo; Roland K. Towery, Cuero (Tex.) Record	Public Service (Ledger); Reporting (separate awards to Brown & Towery)	Attack on corruption in Phoenix City, Ala. (Ledger); coverage of court proceedings involving corruption of Mexican voters (Brown); disclosure of a Veterans Administration land scandal (Towery)
1956	Charles L. Bartlett, Chattanooga (Tenn.) Times	Reporting	Disclosures of improprieties leading to resignation of Harold E. Talbott as Air Force Secretary
1957	*Buford Boone, Tuscaloosa (Ala.) News	Editorial Writing	Stand for upholding the law in a community inflamed by desegregation of the University of Alabama
1958	*Arkansas (Little Rock) Gazette and *Harry Ashmore, Editor	Public Service (Gazette); Editorial Writing (Ashmore)	Coverage of the Little Rock school integration crisis of 1957 (Gazette); stand against racial conflict over school de-

			segregation (Ashmore)
1959	Howard Vann Smith, Miami (Fla.) News; *Ralph McGill, Atlanta (Ga.) Constitution	Reporting (Smith); Editorial Writing (McGill)	Coverage of Florida's migrant workers (Smith); defiance of segregationists (McGill)
1960	*Lenoir Chambers, Norfolk (Va.) Virginian-Pilot; Jack Nelson, Atlanta (Ga.) Constitution	Editorial Writing (Chambers); Reporting (Nelson)	Stand against closing schools in Virginia rather than desegregate (Chambers); exposure of conditions in Georgia's mental institutions (Nelson)
1961	Amarillo (Tex.) Globe-Times	Public Service	Exposure of breakdown in local law enforcement that led to a campaign removing lax officials
1962	Panama City (Fla.) News-Herald; Nathan G. Caldwell and Gene Graham, Nashville (Tenn.) Tennessean	Public Service (News-Herald); Reporting (Caldwell and Graham)	Exposure of numbers-type racket linked to corrupt public officials (News-Herald); disclosure of undercover cooperation between United Mine Workers and management (Caldwell and Graham)
1963	*Ira B. Harkey Jr., Pascagoula (Miss.) Chronicle; Hal Hendrix, Miami (Fla.) News; Oscar Griffin Jr., Pecos (Tex.) Independent & Enterprise	Editorial Writing (Harkey); Reporting (Hendrix and Griffin - separate awards)	Stand against a mob and state authorities that tried to keep a black from integrating the University of Miss. (Harkey); disclosure that the Soviet Union was installing missile launching pads in Cuba (Hendrix);

			disclosure of Billie Sol Estes financial scandal with White House connections (Griffin)
1964	*Hazel Brannon Smith Lexington (Miss.) Advertiser; St. Petersburg (Fla.) Times	Editorial Writing (Smith); Public Service (Times)	Stand in favor of civil rights of blacks & against White Citizen's Councils (Smith); attack on illegal acts of Florida Turnpike Authority (Times)
1965	*John R. Harrison, Gainesville (Fla.) Sun	Editorial Writing	Campaign for better housing primarily for black population
1966	John A. Frasca, Tampa (Fla.) Tribune	Reporting	Disclosure to help free a man wrongfully convicted of robbery
1967	Gene Miller, Miami (Fla.) Herald; *Eugene Patterson, Atlanta (Ga.) Constitution	Reporting (Miller); Editorial Writing (Patterson)	Disclosure of evidence to free two persons wrongfully convicted of murder (Miller); protest against the Georgia legislature's refusal to seat Julian Bond, a black, and reproach of the Joel Chandler Harris Memorial Association (named for creator of Uncle Remus) for anti-black stand (Patterson)
1969	Paul Greenberg, Pine Bluff (Ark.) Commercial	Editorial Writing	Stand against government in Vietnam war

1970	Harold E. Martin, Montgomery (Ala.) Advertiser & Alabama Journal	Reporting	Disclosure of a scheme to use Alabama prisoners for drug experiments
1971	Winston-Salem (N.C.) Journal & Sentinel; *Horance G. Davis Jr., Gainesville (Fla.) Sun	Public Service (Journal & Sentinel); Editorial Writing (Davis)	Blockage of a strip mining operation (Journal & Sentinel); support of peaceful desegregation in local schools (Davis)
1976	Gene Miller, Miami (Fla.) Herald (2nd award)	Reporting	Disclosures that led to exoneration of two men twice sentenced to death
1977	Lufkin (Tex.) News	Public Service	Exposure of abuses in Marine Corp that resulted in death of a recruit.

APPENDIX B

SELECTED ANNOTATED BIBLIOGRAPHY

BOOKS

Agger, Robert E., Daniel Goldrich, and Bert E. Swanson, *The Rulers and the Ruled*. Wiley & Sons Inc.: New York, 1964. Textbook study of the power structure in four American communities.

Carter, Hodding. "Woman Editor's War on Bigots," in *First Person Rural*. Garden City, N.Y.: Doubleday & Co., 1963, pp. 217-225. Profile of Hazel Brannon Smith faced by threats from a White Citizens' Council.

Clark, Thomas D. *The Southern Country Editor*. Indianapolis: Bobbs-Merrill, 1948. Study of the Southern rural press from the 1880's to 1920.

Clark, Thomas D. and Albert D. Kirwan, *The South Since Appomattox: A Century of Regional Change*. New York: Oxford University Press, 1967. Comprehensive survey of economic, political and social changes.

Davis, Cullum, Kathryn Back, and Kay MacLean, *Oral History: From Tape to Tape*. Chicago: American Library Assn., 1977. Easy-to-use oral history guide. East, P.D. *The Magnolia Jungle*. New York: Simon & Schuster, 1960. Unhappy saga of Mississippi editor who defied racial prejudice in *The Petal Paper*.

Emery, Edwin, and Michael Emery, *The Press and America: An Interpretative History of the Mass Media*. 4th Edition, Englewood Cliffs, N.J. Prentice-Hall, 1978. Most recent comprehensive textbook on journalism history; a definitive, detailed work.

Harkey, Ira B. Jr, *The Smell of Burning Crosses*. Harris-Wolfe & Co.: Jacksonville, Ill., 1967. Autobiography of Pulitzer prize winner who defied violent segregationists.

Hohenberg, John. *The Pulitzer Prizes*. New York: Columbia University Press, 1974. History of the awards in books, drama, music and journalism by the administrator of the awards at Columbia University.

Hohenberg, John, ed. *The Pulitzer Prize Story*. New York: Columbia University Press, 1957. Selection of news stories, editorials, cartoons and pictures from the Pulitzer prize exhibits.

Hunter, Floyd. *The Community Power Structure*. Chapel Hill: University of North Carolina Press, 1958. Study of the power structure, including the press, in an area of a half-million population referred to as "Regional City."

Janowitz, Morris. *The Community Press in an Urban Setting*. Glencoe, Ill.: The Free Press, 1952. Study of community press in Chicago based on content analysis and readership surveys.

Jones, Weimar. My Affair with a Weekly. Winston-Salem: John F. Blair, 1960. Selected columns from Jones' weekly newspaper, The Franklin Press in Macon County, N.C.

Kammen, Michael, ed. What is the Good of History? Selected Letters of Carl L. Becker, 1900-1945. Ithaca, N.Y.: Cornell University Press, 1973. Letters from one of America's most philosophical historians including his views on the meaning of history.

Kennedy, Bruce M. Community Journalism - A Way of Life. Ames: Iowa State University Press, 1974. Guidance on operation of a weekly newspaper.

Kirby, Jack T. Media-Made Dixie: The South in the American Imagination. Baton Rouge:Louisiana State University Press, 1978. Examination of the mass media to assess its contribution to the public perceptions of the South.

Lyford, Joseph P. The Talk in Vandalia. New York: Harper & Row, 1965. Part of an investigation of the American character by the Fund for the Republic which presents a portrait of life in a small community.

Marzolf, Marion. Up from the Footnote: A History of Women Journalists. New York: Hastings House, 1977. Study of women's achievements in journalism in spite of sex discrimination.

Frank L. Mott. American Journalism: A History 1690-1960. 3rd Edition. New York: The Macmillan Co., 1962. Outdated but still outstanding text emphasizing the growth of the American newspaper.

Pollard, Edward A. The Lost Cause: A New Southern History of the War of the Confederates. New York: E.B. Treat & Co., 1866. Subscription book account of the Civil War by an opinionated Richmond editor who criticized Jefferson Davis.

Potter, David M. The South and the Sectional Conflict. Baton Rouge: Louisiana State University Press, 1968. Examination of the nature of Southernism including discussion of racial prejudice.

Siebert, Fred, Theodore Peterson, and Wilbur Schramm, Four Theories of the Press. Urbana, Ill.: University Press, 1956. Description of social responsibility theory of American press contrasted with other theories.

Sim, John C. The Grass Roots Press: America's Community Newspapers. Ames: Iowa State University Press, 1969. Study of the decline of the old rural press and the rise of the suburban press.

Woodward, C. Vann. The Burden of Southern History. Baton Rouge: Louisiana State University Press, 1960. Analysis of factors that make the South different from the rest of the nation.

PERIODICALS AND NEWSPAPERS

"Appreciation Day." Newsweek, Dec. 13, 1965, p. 70. Account of counterboycott to aid Hazel Brannon Smith's newspapers.

Bagdikian, B.H. "Death in Silence." Columbia Journalism Review 3:1, Spring 1964, pp. 35-37. Story of Arkansas editor who lost his paper after criticizing local officials.

Beasley, Maurine and Richard R. Harlow, "Coverage of Non-Elites." Grassroots Editor, Fall, 1978, pp. 5-8. Study of Pulitzer prize winners from the community press showing coverage of non-elites usually is limited to a confrontation situation or a crusade.

Edelstein, Alex S. and Joseph J. Contris. "The Public View of the Weekly Newspaper Role." Journalism Quarterly 43, Spring 1966, pp 17-24. Study which finds citizens identify more with community elites who urge consensus than with editors who emphasize controversial change.

Edelstein, Alex and Blaine J. Schulz. "The Weekly Newspaper's Role as Seen by Community Leaders." Journalism Quarterly 40, Fall, 1963, pp. 565-74. Study which shows editors must understand local power structure to succeed in influencing communities.

"George Parr: The Second Duke of Duval." Corpus Christi (Tex.) Caller-Times, April 6-15, 1975. Series detailing corrupt practices of a political boss who controlled a block of Mexican-American votes in Texas.

Harris, T. George. "The 11-Year Siege of Mississippi's Lady Editor." Look, Nov. 16, 1965, pp. 121-28. Profile of Hazel Brannon Smith after she received the Pulitzer prize.

"I Stole '48 Election for LBJ, Former Voting Official Says." Indianapolis (Ind.) Star, July 31, 1977. Front page Associated Press story based on interview with aged election official who contends that George Parr gave orders to "fix" an election that started Lyndon Johnson on his political career.

"In a Madhouse's Din." Newsweek, July 8, 1963, p. 48. Feature on Ira Harkey Jr. and the Pascagoula Chronicle under attack by segregationists.

"Lady's Day." Newsweek, May 16, 1955, p. 70. Report of Pulitzer Prize Award to Caro Brown and Roland K. Towery.

Manger, Karl. "Successful Editor Censors News Bad for the Community." Editor and Publisher, Oct. 12, 1974, p. 16. View of New Jersey editor who refuses to use stories unless they "build" the community.

Martin, H.H. "Tyrant in Texas. Saturday Evening Post, June 26, 1954, pp. 20-1. Profile of George Parr at the time his political empire came under attack.

"Mississippi: Determined Lady." <u>Columbia Journalism Review</u>. 2, Fall, 1963, pp. 37-38. Account of Hazel Brannon Smith's refusal to give in to the White Citizen's Council.

Olien, Clarice N., George A. Donohue, and Phillip Tichenor. "The Community Editor's Power and the Reporting of Conflict." <u>Journalism Quarterly</u>, 45, Summer, 1968, pp. 243-5<. Study of Minnesota community editors which found that the community press tends to protect community institutions rather than report the disruptive side of events.

Rupp, Carla Marie. "Harrison Wears Many Hats as N.Y. Times Group Head." <u>Editor and Publisher</u>, Feb. 28, 1976, pp. 32-33. Description of communications empire headed by John R. Harrison.

"Pulitzer Prizes." Time, May 11, 1953, p. 51. Account of award to Willard Cole and Horance Carter.

Sim, John Cameron. "Community Newspaper Leadership - More Real than Apparent?" <u>Journalism Quarterly</u>. 44, Summer, 1967, pp 276-80. Study that concludes there are no truly effective means of measuring real influences of community newspapers.

UNPUBLISHED MATERIALS

Pulitzer prize exhibits, Columbia University Journalism Library.

Keeshen, Kathleen K. "Journalism's Pulitzer Penwomen." Unpublished paper, University of Maryland College of Journalism, 1978. Background material on all women winners of Pulitzer prizes.

Mueller, Charles W. A Voice of Justice: <u>The Tuscaloosa News Views the Autherine Lucy Incident</u>. Unpublished Master's Thesis, University of Missouri, 1958, Analyzes the activities of the Tuscaloosa News during the admission of Sutherine Lucy to the University of Alabama.

NOTES

1. Edward A. Pollard, The Lost Cause: A New Southern History of the
War of the Confederates (New York: E. B. Treat & Co., 1866), p. 111.

2. Michael Kammen, ed., What is the Good of History? Selected Letters
of Carl L. Becker, 1900-1945 (Ithaca, N.Y.: Cornell University Press,
1973), p. 16. See also Fred Siebert, Theodore Peterson and Wilbur
Schramm, Four Theories of the Press (Urbana, Ill.: University Press,
1956).

3. Kammen, op. cit., p. 157.

4. Marion Marzolf, "American Studies - Ideas for Media Historians."
Journalism History, Vol. 5, No.1, (Spring 1978), Cover, 13-16.

5. Thomas D. Clark and Albert D. Kirwan, The South Since Apomattox: A
Century of Regional Change (New York: Oxford University Press, 1967),
pp. 202-228.

6. Thomas D. Clark, The Southern Country Editor (Indianapolis:
Bobbs-Merrill, 1948), p. 206.

7. Ibid., p. 207.

8. John Hohenberg, The Pulitzer Prizes (New York: Columbia University
Press, 1974). The list of Southern winners is given in Appendix A of
Voices of Change.

9. John Hohenberg, ed., The Pulitzer Prize Story (New York: Columbia
University Press, 1959), p. 69.

10. Clark and Kirwan, op. cit., p. 209.

11. Hohenberg, The Pulitzer Prize Story, pp. 77-79.

12. Ibid., p. 106.

13. Based on 1978 circulation figures.

14. Floyd Hunter, Community Power Structure (Chapel Hill, N.C.: The
University of North Carolina Press, 1953), pp. 181-183.

15. Morris Janowitz, The Community Press in an Urban Setting (Chicago:
University of Chicago Press, 1967), pp. 164-172.

16. Clarine N. Olien, George A. Donohue, and Phillip Tichenor, "The
Community Editor's Power and the Reporting of Conflict." Journalism
Quarterly, 45 (Summer 1968), 242-251.

17. Alex S. Edelstein and Joseph J. Contris, "The Public View of the
Weekly Newspaper Leadership Role." Journalism Quarterly, 43 (1966),
17-24.

142

18.   B. H. Bagdikian, "Death in Silence," <u>Columbia Journalism Review</u> 3:1
(Spring 1964) 35-37, an account of how an Arkansas weekly editor lost his
paper through libel suits after he criticized local officials.   See also
P. D. East, <u>The Magnolia Jungle</u> (New York: Simon & Schuster, 1960), an
autobiography of the editor of a Mississippi weekly which supported
racial justice.

19.   John Cameron Sim, <u>The Grass Roots Press</u> (Ames, Ia.:   Iowa State
University Press, 1969), pp. 106-120.

20.   Karl Manger, "Successful Editor Censors News Bad for the Community."
<u>Editor and Publisher</u>, Oct. 12, 1974, p. 16.

AFL-CIO: 66, 68, 72

Alachua County: 115, 120, 121

Alice (Tex.) Echo: 5, 31, 32

Arkansas Gazette: 3

Arsonists: 89, 123, 124

Ashmore, Harry S.: 3

Atlanta Constitution: 3, 4, 116

Atlanta Journal Constitution: 116

Barnett, Ross: 66, 67

Birmingham, Alabama: 51, 54

Bond, Julian: 4

Boone, Buford: 49, 50

Brown, Alfred: 84, 87

Brown, Caro: 5, 32

Bussing: 118, 122, 123

Butler, Neal: 120

Carter, W. Horace: 7, 8

Chambers, Lenoir: 3

Chicago: 4

Citizens Emergency Unit: 66

Civil War: 1, 2, 52, 70

Cole, Williams: 8

Columbia University: 2

Columbus (Ga.) Enquirer-Sun: 2

Cowles Communications: 97

Davis, Horance G.: 4, 97, 15

Delta Democrat-Times: 3

Des Moines Register Tribune: 98, 102

Duke of Duval: 31

Durant News: 83

Duval County, Tex.: 31, 32, 36

Eisenhower, Dwight D.: 3, 51

Emmer, Phil: 100, 101

Evers, Medgar: 84

FBI: 8, 15, 16, 19, 55, 68

Faubus, Orval: 3

Floggings: 10, 13

Florida Times-Union: 116

Floyd, Jr., Jacob: 32

Gainesville, Florida: 97, 99, 100, 101, 102, 104, 115, 119, 120

Gainesville (Fla.) Sun: 4, 97, 99, 115

Gainesville High School: 121

Grady, Henry: 2

Graham, Dr. Billy: 12

Gulf Coast: 70

Hall, Grover Cleveland: 3

Hamilton, Thomas L.: 12, 13, 16

Harrison, John R.: 4, 97, 116

Harkey, Ira B.:   3, 4, 65

Harris, Julian LaRose: 2

Holmes County, Miss.:   83, 84

Hoover, J. Edgar: 55

Horry County, N.C.:   7, 11, 14, 17

Ingall's Shipyard: 66

Involvement: 54

Jackson County Citizens Emergency Unit: 66, 67, 73

Janowitz, Morris: 3

Jim Wells County (Tex):   32, 36

Johnson, Edward: 115

Johnson, Lyndon B.:   31

Journalism History: 1, 2, 4

Justice Department: 68, 84

King, Martin Luther: 71

Kirk, Claude: 115

Ku Klux Klan: 2, 4, 7, 10, 11, 12, 14, 15, 16, 17, 18, 19, 53, 65, 66, 67

League of Women Voters: 101

Letters to the Editor:

Lexington (Miss.) Advertiser: 3, 83, 84

Lincoln High School: 121

Lucy, Autherine: 49, 51, 52, 53, 54, 56

Macon, Georgia: 50

Macon Telegraph and News: 50

Malone, Vivian: 53

McGill, Ralph: 3

McKinney, Howard: 101, 105

Memphis Commercial Appeal: 2

Meredith, James: 3, 66, 72

Mexican-Americans: 5, 31

Minimum Housing Code: 100, 101, 103, 104

Miami Herald: 116

Minneapolis Star Tribune: 102

Montgomery (Ala.) Advertiser: 3

Myrtle Beach, N.C.:   14, 17

New Orleans Times-Picayune: 66

New York Times: 97, 98, 102, 118

New York Times Newspapers: 97

New York World: 2

Norfolk Virginian-Pilot: 3

Oral History: 5

Oxford, Mississippi:

Parr, George B.:   31, 38

Pascagoula (Miss.) Chronicle: 3, 65, 66, 67, 68

Patterson, Eugene C.:   4

Photojournalism: 104

Pollard, Edward A.:   1, 2

Pulitzer Prizes: 2, 3, 8, 50, 69, 116

Raleigh News Observer: 9

Ramsey, Claude: 66, 67, 72, 74

Ramsey, Dr. Russell: 121

Richmond (Va.) Examiner: 1

Richmond (Va.) Times-Dispatch: 3

Shivers, Allen: 31

Smell of Burning Crosses: 66

Smith, Hazel Brannon: 3, 4, 83, 84, 85

Southern Journalism: 2

Supreme Court, U.S.: 84, 90, 115

Tabor City, N.C.: 7-10, 14

Tabor City (N.C.) Tribune: 3, 4, 7, 8, 10

Texas Rangers: 31, 32

Thomas, Tommy: 122

Today Show: 75

Truman, Harry S.: 11, 12

Turnbow, Hartman: 89-91

Tuscaloosa (Ala.) News: 3, 49,52,54,56

United Nations: 11, 12

University of Alabama: 3, 49, 52, 56, 83, 85

University of Florida: 97, 115, 120

University of Mississippi: 65, 66, 69, 72

University of North Carolina: 9, 11, 14

Urban Renewal Funds: 100

Vietnam: 117, 121

Wallace, George: 53

Walters, Barbara: 75

White Citizens Council: 4, 84, 89, 90

Whiteville (N.C.) News Reporter: 3, 4, 8

World War II: 10, 11, 31, 66, 69, 84, 116

Wright, Rev. T.A.: 119